M000021003

ENGLISH
with a
SMILE

Light-hearted Stories and
Reading Skills for
High-beginning and
Low-intermediate Students

Barbara Zaffran
Staff Development Specialist
in ESL and Native Languages,
New York City

David Krulik
Formerly, Director of ESL Programs,
New York City

National Textbook Company
a division of NTC/CONTEMPORARY PUBLISHING GROUP
Lincolnwood, Illinois USA

To Dany for his cooperation,
Sam Leve for his inspiration,
and my mother, Betty L. Hook,
for her unflagging encouragement
and support

ISBN: 0-8442-0581-8

Published by National Textbook Company,
a division of NTC/Contemporary Publishing Group, Inc.,
4255 West Touhy Avenue,
Lincolnwood (Chicago), Illinois 60646-1975 U.S.A.
©1993 by NTC/Contemporary Publishing Group, Inc.
Manufactured in the United States of America.
Library of Congress Catalog Card Number: 92-60099

8 9 0 VP 9 8 7 6 5

Contents

Introduction   v

Story 1   **Teacher's Pest**   1

Story 2   **Think before You Speak**   9

Story 3   **Speak Faster, Please**   15

Story 4   **Nothing for Nothing**   21

Story 5   **A Big Mouth**   28

Story 6   **The Last Laugh**   35

Story 7   **Honesty Is the Best Policy**   43

Story 8   **Stamp of Approval**   50

Story 9   **Where's the Hitch?**   57

Story 10   **Mismatch**   64

Story 11   **The Picture of Confusion**   71

Story 12   **All Keyed Up**   80

Story 13   **Grand Delusions**   86

Story 14   **A Communication Problem**   95

Story 15   **Inside Out**   101

Story 16   **Which Date Is Which?**   108

Story 17   **The Perfect Arrangement**   114

Story 18   **Problems, Anyone?**   122

Story 19 **If I Knew You Were Coming. . .**   127

Story 20 **Something's Fishy Here**   134

Story 21 **The Greedy Dog**   142

Alphabetized Vocabulary by Page   149

Introduction

To the Student

This is a collection of short stories. Most of the stories talk about students like you. They tell about many interesting people and funny events. Maybe you can see yourself in the stories. Maybe you can think of your own stories to tell or write about.

We hope you enjoy the stories in *English with a Smile*. After you finish this book, we hope you will read *More English with a Smile* as well as many other books. You'll build your English-language skills and have fun as well.

To the Teacher

The stories in this book are based on commonly encountered humorous incidents and experiences. We expect that readers will be able to identify with many of the characters and situations described in the stories.

Each story develops listening, speaking, reading, and writing skills through a communicative approach. Students are asked to take an active part in each chapter by developing personal vocabulary lists, role playing situations based on the stories, contributing prior knowledge, interacting with the characters, and comparing the stories to their feelings and experiences.

There is a structural base to the sequence of stories that can be emphasized at the teacher's discretion. All structures are taken from the stories and are presented in meaningful contexts.

We have taken care to present a variety of activities to foster student-student interaction. In addition, learners will become familiar with various questioning formats often used on tests.

In some instances, proverbs, puns, and idioms have been used as titles or as bases of story plots. You may want students to explore the meanings and usages of the phrases and check their own heritage for similar ideas or sayings.

We sincerely hope that both you and your students enjoy reading the stories and that your students use them as bases for expanding their knowledge of themselves and the English language.

Teacher's Pest

Before You Read

A. What do you think of when you see the word <u>school</u>? Write some words for each category in the map.

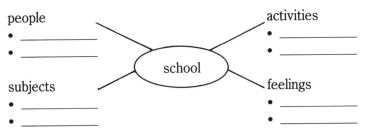

people
• _____
• _____

activities
• _____
• _____

subjects
• _____
• _____

school

feelings
• _____
• _____

Now write four sentences about school using the ideas from your map.

B. Look at the picture on page 3. Answer the questions.

1. What do you see in the picture?
2. What do you think is going to happen?

C. Read these sentences with a partner. Can you guess the meanings of the underlined words? Use a dictionary if you need help.

Definitions

1. Josie <u>agrees</u> to be the teacher.

   _____

2. Mr. Rula is <u>annoyed</u> with Josie because she doesn't listen to him.

   _____

1

Definitions

3. Sit down and be <u>quiet</u>!   _____
4. Come to the <u>front</u> of the
    room and be the teacher.   _____
5. Josie isn't quiet, but Mr.
    Rula <u>continues</u> with the
    lesson. He doesn't stop.   _____
6. I don't want to hear a word
    from anyone. <u>Everyone</u>, be
    quiet.   _____

7. Josie <u>gets up</u> from her seat.   _____

8. It is <u>hot</u> in the summer.   _____

9. Quiet! Stop making <u>noise</u>!   _____

10. Josie <u>talks</u> to a friend.   _____

D. Match the synonyms (words that have the same meaning).

A	B
1. gets up	a. doesn't stop
2. continues	b. speak
3. quiet	c. a little angry
4. annoyed	d. stands
5. talk	e. silent

Teacher's Pest

It is June. The sun is in the sky. It is very hot. Josie is tired of
school. She wants to be at the beach. She cannot sit in her seat.
She cannot stop talking. While the teacher writes on the board,
Josie gets up and talks to a friend. The teacher, Mr. Rula, hears
the noise and says, "Josie, sit down and be quiet." Josie sits down.
Mr. Rula continues with the lesson. Josie gets up and talks to
another friend. "Sit down and be quiet," says Mr. Rula. He is very
annoyed with her. Josie continues talking.

"O.K.," says Mr. Rula, "if you want to talk, then come to the
front of the classroom and be the teacher."

"All right," agrees Josie. She comes to the front of the
classroom and says, "Quiet, everyone. I am the new teacher, and I
say 'class dismissed.'"

While You Read

A. 1. Write notes about the story.

month	_____
weather	_____, _____
teacher	hot, _____, _____
students	tired, _____, _____, _____

Use your notes to help you write a paragraph about Josie's story.

2. Now write ideas for a new story.

month	_____
weather	_____, _____, _____
teacher	_____, _____, _____
students	_____, _____, _____

Use your notes to help you write a new story.

3. Compare your story with the story about Josie.

	the story about Josie	your story
month		
weather		
teacher		
students		

Now find a partner. Tell your partner about your chart.

B. Think about these questions while you read. Then answer the questions.

1. Why do you think Josie is a pest?
2. What happens after Josie says "class dismissed"?
3. How do you think Mr. Rula feels?
4. Do you think Mr. Rula's idea was a good one? Why or why not?
5. Do you think Josie is a good student? Why or why not?

Sit in groups of three. Ask each other questions 1 through 5 and write the answers in the chart on page 6. Share your group's answers with the class.

	Student 1	Student 2	Student 3
Josie is a pest because . . .			
After Josie says "class dismissed". . .			
Mr. Rula feels . . .			
Mr. Rula's idea was/ wasn't a good one because . . .			
Josie is a good/bad student because . . .			

After You Read

Comprehension Check

A. Match column A with column B to make sentences about the story.

A	**B**
1. The sun is	a. tired of school.
2. Josie is	b. very annoyed.
3. She cannot	c. to be the teacher.
4. Mr. Rula is	d. in the sky.
5. He asks her	e. stop talking.
6. She tells the class	f. to go home.

B. Complete the story. Then check your work with a partner.

It _____ June. The _____ is in the sky. It is very

_____. Josie is _____ of school. She _____ to

be at the beach. She cannot sit in her _____. She cannot

stop _____. While the _____ writes on the board,

Josie gets up and _____ to a friend. The teacher, Mr. Rula,

hears the _____ and says, ''Josie, _____

_____ and be quiet.'' Josie _____ down. Mr. Rula

_____ with the lesson. Josie _____ _____ and

talks to another _____. ''Sit down and be _____,''

says Mr. Rula. He is very _____ with her. Josie

_____ talking.

"O.K.," says Mr. Rula, "if you _____ to talk, then come

to the _____ of the classroom and be the teacher."

"All right," _____ Josie. She comes to the front of the

_____ and says, ''_____, everyone. I _____

the new teacher, and I say 'class _____.' ''

C. You are Mr. Rula. Write a letter to Josie's mother. Tell her
about Josie.

Dear _____,

_____

_____

_____

Sincerely,

Mr. Rula

Structure Practice

A. Write a complete sentence for each group of words. Add any missing words and punctuation. Look at the story if you need help.

1. sun / is / sky

2. teacher / writes / board

3. she / wants / be / beach

4. Josie / gets / talks / friend

5. come / front / classroom

B. Complete the sentences. Follow the example. Make any necessary changes.

Example: You are interested in school.

1. They _____

2. He _____

3. I _____

4. We _____

5. She _____

Now choose one of these verbs: *sit down, get up, agree, talk.* Write a sentence with the verb. Show it to a partner. Ask your partner to make five new sentences by changing the subject of the sentence.

C. Write the imperative form for each sentence.

Example: The teacher tells Josie to sit down.
    "Sit down, Josie."

1. Josie tells the class to be quiet.
2. Mr. Rula tells Josie to come to the front of the room.
3. The teacher tells the students to study for the test.
4. Rosemary tells Josie to stop talking.
5. Mr. Rula tells Josie to write the answers on the board.

Story 2

Think before You Speak

Before You Read

A. What do you think of when you see the word <u>airport</u>? Write some words for each category in the map.

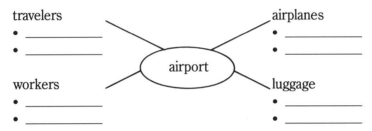

travelers
• _____
• _____

airplanes
• _____
• _____

airport

workers
• _____
• _____

luggage
• _____
• _____

Now write four sentences about airports using the ideas from your map.

B. Look at the picture on page 10. Answer the questions.

1. What do you see in the picture?
2. What do you think is going to happen?

C. Match each word or phrase with its meaning. Use a dictionary if you need help.

1. to check in
2. difficult

3. to be upset
4. scale
5. to take one's time

a. to go slowly
b. a machine that tells how heavy something is
c. to register
d. to be worried about something
e. not easy

D. Read the story. Write the words you don't know. Then work with a partner to guess the meanings of the words. Use the story for help. Use a dictionary to check your work.

Words	Definitions
————	————————————
————	————————————
————	————————————
————	————————————
————	————————————
————	————————————
————	————————————
————	————————————
————	————————————
————	————————————

Think before You Speak

1 Maria is sixteen years old. She has long brown hair and green eyes. She's five feet two inches tall and very thin. Maria is waiting in line at the airport in Santo Domingo. She is leaving her native country to live with her sister in the United States. She speaks English very well. Even though she loves her sister, it is very difficult for her to leave her homeland. All her family and friends live in Santo Domingo. In the United States she has no friends. Her eyes are full of tears. Suddenly, she hears:

2 "Who is next, please? Come on, where's the luggage?"

It is the airline employee telling her to pick up her luggage and put it on the scale. Maria pulls and pulls, but her suitcase is too heavy. She can't pick it up. No one tries to help her.

The man in back of her is very impatient. He, too, is waiting to check in his luggage. He is in a hurry to get a good seat on the plane.

"What's wrong with these teenagers? Why are they never in a hurry? Why aren't they able to help themselves? Look at this girl here. Why is she taking her time? When is she going to move? I'm tired. I'm in a hurry to get a good seat, to sit down, and to relax."

3 Maria is very angry at the man. But she is very polite, and in her best English she says:

"Why are you so upset? Where are you running? There are enough seats for everyone on the plane. If you're in such a hurry, why don't you help me pick up my suitcase? It is much too heavy for me."

The man is surprised to hear Maria speak English. He quickly picks up her suitcase, puts it on the scale, and turns the other way. He is too embarrassed to look at her.

While You Read

A. 1. As you read, take notes and fill in the charts.

Maria

age	
how she looks	
native country	
language(s)	
how she feels	
problem	

Man

age	
how he looks	
how he feels	
what he does first	
what he does later	

2. Use your notes to help you write a paragraph about Maria and a paragraph about the man. You can give the man a name.

B. Read the story again. Stop after each section to answer the question.

Section 1. Why is it difficult for Maria to leave Santo Domingo?
Section 2. How do you feel about the man in back of Maria? Why?
Section 3. Why is the man embarrassed?

After You Read

Comprehension Check

A. Number these sentences so they tell the story about Maria and the man. Then check your work with a partner.

_____ Maria is angry. She asks the man to help her.
_____ She is leaving Santo Domingo to live with her sister in the United States.
_____ The man helps her. He is surprised to hear Maria speak English.
_____ At the airport an impatient man complains about Maria in English.
_____ Maria is sixteen years old.

B. Choose the best word to complete each sentence.

1. Maria has long _____ hair.
   a. red b. brown c. blond

2. It is _____ for her to leave her homeland.
   a. fun b. easy c. difficult

3. Maria's suitcase is too _____.
   a. big b. light c. heavy

4. The man in back of Maria is very _____.
   a. small b. impatient c. polite

5. Maria _____ English very well.
   a. speaks b. reads c. writes

C. Surprise! The man sits next to Maria on the plane. What do they say to each other? Act out the situation with a partner.

Structure Practice

A. Change these sentences to the present progressive form.

> **Example:** I go to school every day.
> I <u>am going</u> to school now.

1. Maria waits in line at the airport. (now)
2. The airport employee tells her to pick up her luggage. (now)
3. Maria's plane leaves at 9:00. (now)
4. The man picks up Maria's suitcase. (now)
5. Maria sits in her seat. (now)

B. Make questions for these answers.

> **Example:** Maria is sixteen years old.
> <u>How</u> old is Maria?

1. Maria is five feet two inches tall. (How)
2. Maria and her family are from Santo Domingo. (Where)
3. Rosa is Maria's sister. (Who)
4. Maria is upset because the man is complaining about her. (Why)
5. The airplane is white. (What color)

C. Complete each sentence with **a, an,** or **the.**

1. Maria is at _____ airport in Santo Domingo.

2. The man wants _____ good seat on the plane.

3. A man wants to wash his hands. He asks, "Where is _____ men's room?"

4. Maria is _____ girl.

5. I like to fly in _____ airplane.

Story 3

Speak Faster, Please

Before You Read

A. What do you think of when you see the word <u>tourist</u>? Write some words for each category in the map.

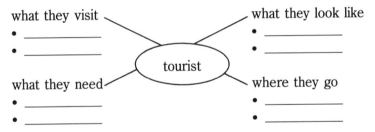

what they visit
* _____
* _____

tourist

what they need
* _____
* _____

what they look like
* _____
* _____

where they go
* _____
* _____

Now use your ideas to write four sentences about tourists in the United States or in your native country.

B. Look at the picture on page 17. Answer the questions.

1. Think of five words that describe the man with the camera. Use the words to write a short paragraph about the man.
2. What are the boy and girl doing?
3. What do you think the man is saying?
4. Read the title of the story. What do you think the story is going to be about?

C. Choose the correct definition for each word. Use a dictionary if you need help.

1. tourist   a. tower   b. visitor   c. native
2. huge   a. very tall   b. very big   c. very heavy
3. lucky   a. fortunate   b. ugly   c. bad
4. metro   a. city   b. metropolis   c. train in Paris
5. embarrassed   a. surprised   b. happy   c. ashamed

D. Read the story. Write the words you don't know. Then work with a partner to guess the meanings of the words. Use the story for help. Use a dictionary to check your work.

Words	**Definitions**
_____	_____
_____	_____
_____	_____
_____	_____
_____	_____
_____	_____
_____	_____
_____	_____
_____	_____

Speak Faster, Please

1   Ray is studying in France for the year. He speaks French very well and has many French friends. One day, while Ray is drinking coffee with his French girlfriend in a little cafe, a man comes over to them. The man looks like a tourist. He is wearing a bright colored shirt and shorts. He has a huge camera hanging around his neck.

"How—do—I—get—to—the—Eiffel—Tower?" he asks very slowly and loudly.

Ray looks at him strangely and answers him.

2 "Take the metro to Trocadero, and you're there."

The man continues speaking slowly and loudly.

"You—speak—English—very—well. How—many—years—have—you—been—studying—it?"

"Twenty years."

"Where?" the man yells.

"In Chicago."

3 "Why?"

"Because I'm American. You can stop talking slowly and loudly now."

"Oh, I see. You're lucky to be bilingual."

The man is very embarrassed.

While You Read

A. While you read, take notes and complete this chart. Not all the answers are in the story. You must also look at the picture and think.

	Ray	**Tourist**
where he lives now		
what language he speaks		
age		
nationality		
clothes		
how he feels		

Use your notes to write a paragraph about Ray and a paragraph about the tourist.

B. Read the story again. Stop after each section to answer the question.

Section 1. Do you think all tourists are like this man? Explain your answer.

Section 2. Why does the man speak slowly and loudly?

Section 3. Why is the tourist embarrassed?

After You Read

Comprehension Check

A. Write **T** if the sentence is true and **F** if the sentence is false. Correct the sentence if it is false.

1. Ray is studying in Spain for two years.
2. Ray is having lunch with his girlfriend.
3. A tourist asks Ray a question.

4. The man speaks slowly and loudly.
5. Ray is French.

B. Think about the story. Write words in this chart that help you remember the story. If you need help, look at the story.

place	
characters (people in the story)	
action	
ending	

Use your notes to help you write a summary of the story.

C. You are standing on a busy street corner in your neighborhood. A tourist asks you for directions. Role-play the conversation with a partner.

D. A tourist comes to your native country. What are some interesting places to visit? Why? Bring pictures to show your friends.

Structure Practice

A. Change these sentences to the simple present tense.

Example: I am studying English now. (every day)
          I <u>study</u> English every day.

1. Ray is studying in France for the year. (every night)
2. We are drinking coffee with our friends now. (four times a week)

3. She is wearing shorts. (when it's hot)
4. George is speaking loudly now. (all the time)
5. They are visiting their relatives today. (every Sunday)

B. Make information questions for these answers.

Example: Ray likes to drink coffee.
<u>What</u> does Ray like to drink?

1. Ray speaks French very well. (How)
2. They live in France. (Where)
3. Ray and his girlfriend drink coffee in a cafe. (Where)
4. You get on the metro at nine o'clock every day. (What time)
5. We like to talk with tourists. (With whom)

C. Underline the adverbs and adjectives in the story and write them in the lists below.

Example: Ray is drinking <u>hot</u> coffee and talking <u>excitedly</u> to his girlfriend.

Adverbs (tell about a verb)
  excitedly

Adjectives (tell about a noun)
  hot

Nothing for Nothing

Before You Read

A. What do you think of when you see the phrase <u>to wait in line</u>? Write some words for each category in the map.

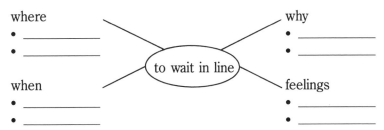

where
• _____
• _____

when
• _____
• _____

to wait in line

why
• _____
• _____

feelings
• _____
• _____

Now show your map to a partner. Ask your partner to write four sentences using your ideas. Then read your partner's sentences. Do you want to change anything? Do you want to add anything? Share the sentences with the class.

B. Look at the picture on page 23. Answer the questions.

1. What do you see in the picture?
2. What do you think is going to happen?

C. Read these sentences with a partner. Can you guess the meanings of the underlined words? Use a dictionary if you need help.

Definitions

1. Mrs. Dale is sitting in a wheelchair. An airport attendant <u>approaches</u> her and tells her she must pay to use the wheelchair.

_____

21

Definitions

2. Mrs. Dale is loud and
    impatient. Her behavior is
    bad.   _____

3. Mrs. Dale must pay five
    dollars to use the
    wheelchair. There is a $5.00
    charge.   _____

4. Mrs. Dale is never happy.
    She complains a lot.   _____

5. Mrs. Dale keeps annoying
    her husband. Mr. Dale
    finally says, "Leave me
    alone."   _____

6. Mr. Dale is embarrassed by
    his wife's behavior. He turns
    around and pretends not to
    know her.   _____

7. Mrs. Dale isn't satisfied with
    what she has. She wants
    more and more.   _____

8. Mrs. Dale doesn't see any
    place to sit down. There are
    no seats.   _____

9. Mrs. Dale doesn't speak in a
    quiet voice. She shouts.   _____

10. John's legs are broken. He
    cannot walk, so he uses a
    wheelchair.   _____

D. Match each word with its meaning.

1. satisfied	a. fee
2. charge	b. yell
3. pretend	c. happy
4. shout	d. come near
5. approach	e. imagine

Nothing For Nothing

Mr. and Mrs. Dale live in Los Angeles, California. They live on Main Street, at number 1978. It is a pretty street with many trees and flowers in front of the houses. Mrs. Dale isn't satisfied with what she has. She wants to travel and see new things.

"Let's go to Portugal! Let's go to Spain or India or China. Let's go somewhere, but let's leave Los Angeles," Mrs. Dale tells her husband.

After many days of listening to his wife, Mr. Dale says angrily:

"Stop it. Stop annoying me. O.K. I'm buying tickets for China, just leave me alone."

Finally, the big day arrives. Mr. and Mrs. Dale go to the airport and wait in a long line to check in their luggage. Mrs. Dale, forever a pest, begins to complain to her husband.

"Do we have to stand in line? Do you see any seats? Why is there a long line? Find a seat for me now! I don't feel well."

Mr. Dale is embarrassed by his wife's behavior. He pretends not to know her. When he turns around to tell his wife to be quiet, she isn't there.

Suddenly a lady in a wheelchair calls out to him:

"Come here, Jim, and push me."

Mr. Dale pretends not to hear her.

Mrs. Dale continues shouting.

An airport attendant approaches her and tells her there is a $5.00 charge for the use of the wheelchair.

When Jim Dale turns around again, his wife is next to him.

"You don't feel well. Go sit down. I can check in the luggage."

"That's O.K., dear. I feel much better now. I can stand with you until we check our luggage."

While You Read

A. As you read, take notes and fill in the chart.

main characters	
where they go	
why they go	
problem	
ending	

Now use your notes to write a summary of the story.

B. Read the story again. Underline each new word you find. Then rewrite the sentences using a synonym or a group of words in place of the underlined words.

After You Read

Comprehension Check

A. Answer the questions.

1. What words describe Mrs. Dale?
2. What words describe Mr. Dale?
3. Do you think Mrs. Dale is really sick? Explain your answer.
4. Why does Mrs. Dale get out of the wheelchair?
5. Do you think the Dales will enjoy their trip? Why or why not?

B. Number these sentences so they tell the story about Mr. and Mrs. Dale. Then check your work with a partner.

_____ Mrs. Dale finds a wheelchair to sit in.

_____ Mr. Dale buys tickets to China.

_____ Mrs. Dale says she feels better.

_____ Mrs. Dale says she doesn't feel well.

_____ Mr. and Mrs. Dale go to the airport.

_____ Mrs. Dale wants to leave Los Angeles.

C. Match column **A** with column **B** to make sentences about the story.

A	**B**
1. Mrs. Dale	a. a wheelchair.
2. At the airport	b. complains a lot.
3. She finds	c. tells her there's a $5.00 charge.
4. The airport attendant	d. so she suddenly feels better.
5. She doesn't want to pay,	e. she pretends to be sick.

D. Imagine you are coming to America. Tell about leaving your country. Why are you leaving? Who is going with you? What are you taking? Describe the airport or the port. How do you feel? What happens on your trip? Where do you arrive? Who meets you?

Structure Practice

A. Choose the best preposition to complete each sentence.

from   on   in   to   at   for

1. Mrs. Dale lives _____ Los Angeles.

2. She and her husband live _____ Main Street

    _____ number 1978.

3. They want to take a trip _____ China.

4. They live far away _____ the airport.

5. Find a seat _____ me, please.

B. Choose the best answer for each question.

1. Where do Mr. and Mrs. Dale live?
   a. They are living in Los Angeles.
   b. They live in Los Angeles.

2. Why are they standing in line?
   a. They stand in line to check in their luggage.
   b. They are standing in line to check in their luggage.

3. Where are Mr. and Mrs. Dale going?
   a. They are going to China.
   b. They go to China.

4. Who calls out from the wheelchair?
   a. Mrs. Dale is calling out from the wheelchair.
   b. Mrs. Dale calls out from the wheelchair.

5. How does Mrs. Dale feel at the end of the story?
   a. She is feeling better now.
   b. She feels better.

C. Write the imperative form of each sentence. Remember to be polite!

Examples: Mrs. Dale wants to travel.

"Let's travel," says Mrs. Dale.

Mr. Dale wants his wife to help him carry the luggage.

"Help me carry the luggage, please," says Mr. Dale.

1. Mr. Dale wants to go to China.
2. Mr. Dale tells his wife to stop annoying him.
3. Mrs. Dale wants her husband to find a seat for her.
4. Mrs. Dale needs someone to push her wheelchair.
5. Mr. Dale doesn't want his wife to stand next to him.

A Big Mouth

Before You Read

A. What do you think of when you see the word <u>teacher</u>? Write some words in the map.

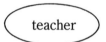

teacher

Now write three sentences about teachers using the ideas from your map.

B. Look at the picture on page 31. Answer the questions.

1. What do you see? Write three sentences that tell about the picture.
2. How do you think the boy feels?
3. What do you think is going to happen?

C. Do you know what these words mean? Talk about their meanings with a partner. Then use a dictionary to check your work.

to adjust	to notice
definitely	to pick on
great	problem
hate	schedule
nearly	teenager

D. Use the words in activity C to complete these sentences. Change the form of a word if necessary.

1. At first everything is new and different. Then we

   _____ and begin to feel comfortable.

2. One day Fred _____ a new student in his

   English class.

3. I have some _____ at school. The work is difficult

   because I don't understand English very well.

4. If I talk to my friends, the teacher gives me a zero. But he

   never gives other students zeros. He _____ me.

5. Everything is just _____! My teachers are

   excellent, and I love my new school.

6. I have a class at nine o'clock, so I _____ can't meet

   you then. How about another time?

7. Fred is 16 and Mara is 15. They are _____.

8. Fred has an easy _____: three classes, then gym,

   then lunch, then two more classes.

9. Fred has six classes. Mara is in five of his classes. She is

   in _____ all of his classes.

10. My teacher picks on me, so I _____ him. I don't

    like him at all.

A Big Mouth

It's the first week of school. Fred is a new student and he doesn't know anyone. After a few weeks, he notices that one girl is in nearly all of his classes. He decides to make friends with her.

"Hi, my name is Fred Shamah. What's yours?"

"Mara Chavez."

"I'm new to this school, and I really don't know many people. I notice that you're in nearly all of my classes, and so maybe we can be friends. How were your first few weeks?"

"Just great. I'm new here, too. I have excellent teachers. My uncle teaches here, so it was easy for me to adjust. He was a big help to me. Was it hard to get used to your new schedule?"

"No. The schedule was easy to get used to, but I have another problem. There's one teacher who just doesn't like me. He picks on me all the time. He tells me to stand in the corner if I call out. He takes me to the dean if I forget my homework. He even calls my mother if I fail a test."

"He sounds like he cares a lot about you."

"No, he doesn't. He hates me, and I hate him, too. Do you know what I did? I wrote a letter and told him I hated him, that he wasn't a nice person and definitely did not understand teenagers. I asked the dean to put me in a different class. And I put chewing gum on my teacher's chair this morning. Well, let's not talk about school. What are you doing tonight?"

"I'm going to visit my Uncle Burt. Why don't you come with me? Maybe he can help you with your problems at school. I live at 672 John Street. Come over at 8:00 P.M."

"Thanks. That's a good idea, Mara. See you at 8:00."

Later that evening, Fred and Mara meet and walk over to her uncle's house. Mara rings the bell, and a man answers the door.

"Hi, Uncle Burt!"

"Hello, Mr. Chavez?"

Fred is surprised and embarrassed. He did not expect to see the teacher he hates.

While You Read

A. Find these sentences in the story.
   1. Write the sentence that tells that Fred doesn't have many friends.

2. Write the sentences that tell about Fred's problem.
3. Write the sentences that tell what Fred did to his teacher.
4. Write the sentence that tells how Fred feels when he sees Uncle Burt.

B. As you read, take notes and fill in the chart.

main characters	
place	
problem	
action	
ending	

Sit with a partner. Use your notes to tell the story to your partner. Then tell what you think happens next.

After You Read

Comprehension Check

A. Answer these questions about the story.

1. Why does Fred ask Mara to be friends with him?
2. Why was it easy for Mara to adjust?
3. Why is it difficult for Fred to adjust?
4. Where do Fred and Mara go?
5. Who is Uncle Burt?

B. Sit in groups of four. Talk about why Fred asked Mara to be friends with him. Is this a good reason to choose a friend? Ask your group.

	Student 1	Student 2	Student 3	Student 4
Yes				
No				

Group decision: _____

With your group, decide on four good reasons to choose a friend. Share them with the class.

C. Complete the story. Then check your work with a partner.

Fred is a new _____. He notices that one _____ is

in nearly all of his _____. Fred tells her that his

_____ is easy, but there's one _____ he doesn't like.

Mara invites him to _____ her Uncle Burt. Later that

_____, Fred and Mara walk over to her _____ house.

Her uncle is Fred's _____.

Structure Practice

A. Complete the sentences with the past tense of the verb <u>to be</u>.

Example: Fred <u>was</u> a new student.

1. How _____ your first few weeks of school?

2. _____ it hard to get used to your new school? No, it

_____.

3. Fred and Mara _____ in the same classes.

4. I _____ very happy with my teachers, _____
you?

5. He _____ a nice person.

B. Complete each sentence with the past tense of the verb in
parentheses.

Examples: a. Where <u>did</u> you <u>go</u> last evening? (go)
           b. Mara <u>liked</u> her teachers. (like)

1. I _____ him that I hated him. (tell)

2. Fred _____ chewing gum on the chair. (put)

3. They _____ a letter to the teacher. (write)

4. What _____ you _____ in class? (do)

5. Fred _____ not _____ his teacher. (like)

C. Change these sentences to the negative form. Use contractions wherever you can.

Example: It was the first week of school.
                  It <u>wasn't</u> the first week of school.

1. Mara and Fred <u>were</u> new students.
2. It <u>is</u> easy to make friends.
3. I <u>am</u> going to visit my uncle.
4. It <u>was</u> hard for me to get used to my schedule.
5. We <u>are</u> working hard this year.

Story 6

The Last Laugh

Before You Read

A. What do you think of when you see the word <u>trick</u>? Write some words in the map.

Now write three sentences about tricks using the ideas from your map.

B. Look at the picture on page 37. Answer the questions.

1. What do you see in the picture?
2. What do you think is going to happen?

C. Read these sentences with a partner. Can you guess the meanings of the underlined words? Use a dictionary if you need help.

Definitions

1. George and Jack <u>exchanged</u> places. George took Jack's place in class, and Jack took George's place.

_____

2. No one knew we exchanged places. We <u>fooled</u> everyone.

_____

35

Definitions

3. George and Jack are
    handsome boys. They are
    very good-looking.   _____

4. George and Jack look exactly
    the same. They are identical
    twins.   _____

5. Susan opened the door.
    Water from a pail fell on her
    head. Philip laughed. He
    played a practical joke on
    Susan.   _____

6. A slim person is not fat.   _____

7. Jack stuttered, "Um, um,
    um, I d-d-don't know the,
    the, um, story."   _____

8. Mr. Daniels asked Jack to
    summarize a story. Jack told
    the story in a few sentences.   _____

9. No one can tell George and
    Jack apart. They look exactly
    alike.   _____

10. George and Jack are twins.
    They are the same age and
    they have the same mother.   _____

D. Match the antonyms (words that have the opposite meanings).

A	B
1. handsome	a. fat
2. identical	b. to speak smoothly
3. to keep for yourself	c. ugly
4. to stutter	d. to exchange
5. slim	e. different

The Last Laugh

1

George and Jack were identical twins. They looked so much alike that no one was able to tell them apart. The twins did everything together. They played ball together; they watched television together; they studied together; and they even walked to school together because they attended the same school.

George and Jack were both six feet tall. Their hair was black and their eyes were brown. They were slim, handsome, and smart. However, there was one problem. They liked practical jokes.

One day George said to Jack: "Let's dress exactly alike today."

"Why do you want to do that?" asked Jack.

"I have a good idea for a practical joke. When we dress alike, no one can tell us apart. Let's exchange class schedules and fool everybody. I am Jack for today, and you are George. O.K.?"

"That sounds like fun. Let's do it," said Jack.

2

So the brothers exchanged schedules for the day. Everything started out all right, but soon strange things began to happen. Mrs. Sayag asked George to do a math problem at the board using a method George did not know.

Meanwhile, in English class, Mr. Daniels asked Jack to summarize the short story that the class studied for homework. Jack stuttered and stammered, and was very embarrassed.

"Why didn't you do your homework, George? Do you have a good reason?" asked Mr. Daniels.

Jack almost said: "I'm not George, I'm Jack," but then he remembered why he was in all this trouble. So he just said: "Excuse me, sir, but my brother asked me to do something for him."

3

At lunch, Mr. Daniels and Mrs. Sayag discussed the twins' strange behavior. They realized that the twins played a trick on them. The teachers decided to play a trick of their own. They arranged for the twins' afternoon teachers to give difficult surprise quizzes.

The next day Jack's history teacher called to him after class. "Why did you fail this quiz, Jack?" he asked him.

George's French teacher asked: "Why did you fail this quiz, George?"

The boys answered: "We wanted to have a good laugh, so we exchanged places. However, we see now that although we laughed a little, we didn't have the last laugh."

While You Read

A. 1. Complete this time line to show the order of the events in the story.

Action 1:   Action 2:   Action 3:   Action 4:   Action 5:
George and   George and   The teachers   The teachers   George and
Jack decided   Jack ...   realized ...   ...   Jack ...
to ...

2. Share your time line with a partner. Then take turns telling the story about George and Jack. Use your time lines for help.

B. 1. Read the story again. Stop after each section to answer the questions.

Section 1. What idea does George have? Do you think it's a good idea? Why or why not?

Section 2. What happened to George and Jack in class? How did they feel?

Section 3. What did the teachers do? How do you think the teachers felt?

2. Do you think George and Jack want to exchange places again? Explain your answer.

After You Read

Comprehension Check

A. Complete this section of the story. Then check your work with a partner.

George and Jack were identical _____. They looked so

much alike that no one was able to _____ them apart. The

twins did everything _____. They played _____

together; they watched television together; they _____

together; and they even walked to _____ together because

they _____ the same school.

George and Jack were both _____ feet tall. Their hair was

black and their _____ were brown. They were slim,

_____, and smart. However, there was _____

problem. They liked _____ _____.

One day George said to Jack: "Let's _____ exactly alike today."

"Why do you _____ to do that?" asked Jack.

"I have a good _____ for a practical joke. When we dress alike, no one can tell us _____. Let's _____ class schedules and _____ everybody. I am Jack for _____, and you are George. O.K.?"

"That sounds like _____. Let's do it," said Jack.

B. Think about the story. Complete this chart. Write words that help you remember the story. If you need help, look at the story.

who the story is about	
what they did	
when they did it	
when their problem began	
what happened to them	
how the story ended	

Now use your notes in the chart to help you write a summary of the story.

C. Talk or write about these questions.

1. Did you ever play a practical joke? If so, what was it? What happened?
2. April 1 is called April Fool's Day in the United States. On this day, people play tricks on each other. Is there a day like this in your native country? If so, tell about it.
3. What do you think Jack's history teacher and George's French teacher will do next? What would you do if you were the teacher?

Structure Practice

A. Write the past tense form of each verb. Then write a sentence using each verb in the past tense.

1. to look
2. to exchange
3. to ask
4. to study
5. to watch

B. Complete the sentences. Then write a question for each sentence. Begin each question with <u>why</u>.

1. George and Jack walked to school together because _____.

2. George and Jack dressed alike because _____.

3. George couldn't do the math problem because _____.

4. The boys failed their quizzes because _____.

5. George and Jack exchanged places because _____.

C. Complete these sentences with the correct form of the verb <u>to</u> <u>say</u>.

1. I have nothing _____.

2. "I called you, but you didn't hear me," _____ Jack.

3. If you listen to what your teacher _____ every day, you will be a good student.

4. He didn't listen to what the teacher was _____, so he didn't know what to study.

5. We _____ hello to each other every morning.

Honesty Is the Best Policy

Before You Read

A. What do you think of when you see the word <u>test</u>? Write some words in the map.

Now write three sentences about tests using the ideas from your map.

B. Look at the picture on page 45. Answer the questions.

1. What do you see in the picture?
2. What do you think is going to happen?

C. Match each word or phrase with its meaning. Use a dictionary if you need help.

1. to announce	a. to tell someone to be careful
2. to cheat	b. to move around
3. to warn	c. to say something important
4. to concentrate	d. to be dishonest
5. to wander	e. to think about one thing

43

D. Read the story. Write the words you don't know. Then work with a partner to guess the meanings of the words. Use the story for help. Use a dictionary to check your work.

Words	Definitions
_____	_____
_____	_____
_____	_____
_____	_____
_____	_____
_____	_____
_____	_____
_____	_____
_____	_____

Honesty Is the Best Policy

1   Elena was not a good student. Her head was in the clouds most of the time. She wanted to listen in class and to study, but other things were more important: her boyfriend, her clothes, her hairstyle, and television. Every time she tried to concentrate on her lesson, her mind wandered.

2   One day, her English teacher, Mrs. Frederickson, announced an important test. She reviewed all week. Where was Elena? She seemed to be there, but her mind was absent.

"Did you copy the questions? Did you do the exercises? Did you write your homework? Elena, wake up! You're going to fail the test," warned Mrs. Frederickson.

3   The day of the test arrived. Elena didn't study very much, and she didn't know many questions. She tried to guess but soon gave up.

Next to Elena sat Ivan, a very serious student. Elena didn't want to fail the test, so she decided to cheat. She knew it was wrong, but she was desperate. She began to copy all of Ivan's answers.

4   Ivan noticed Elena cheating and was very angry. Quickly he changed all his answers so that they were incorrect. So did Elena. Then, hiding his paper, he quickly changed his answers back to the way they were. Elena wasn't quick enough and the bell rang. Ivan turned to Elena and laughed.

"Honesty is the best policy," he said. "Now *all* your answers are wrong for sure."

While You Read

A. While you read, complete this chart. Put an X in the "yes" or "no" column for each person. Not all the answers are in the story. You must also look at the picture and think.

	Elena		Ivan	
	yes	no	yes	no
is a good student				
is a girl				
studied a lot for the test				
knows the answers				
is cheating on the test				
feels desperate				
feels angry				
will pass the test				

B. Read the story again. Stop after each section to answer the question.

Section 1. Why wasn't Elena a good student?

Section 2. What did Mrs. Frederickson do?

Section 3. What did Elena do?

Section 4. What did Ivan do?

After You Read

Comprehension Check

A. Write **T** if the sentence is true and **F** if the sentence is false. Correct the sentence if it is false.

1. Elena's head was in the clouds.
2. When she tried to concentrate, her mind wandered.
3. She studied very hard for her English test.
4. She knew it was wrong, so she didn't cheat.
5. Honesty is the best policy.

B. Choose the best answer to complete each sentence.
1. The most important thing to Elena was _____.
   a. her studies
   b. school
   c. her boyfriend

2. Mrs. Frederickson warned Elena to study because _____.
   a. she cared a lot
   b. she didn't like Elena
   c. she wanted Elena to fail

3. Ivan sat _____ Elena.
   a. behind
   b. next to
   c. in front of

4. Ivan _____ all the answers.
   a. knew
   b. didn't know
   c. guessed

5. Elena learned that _____.
   a. it's good to cheat
   b. crime pays
   c. honesty is the best policy

C. Mrs. Frederickson hears Ivan talking to Elena after the bell
rings. She asks the two students what is happening. In groups
of three, talk about what Ivan and Elena will say to Mrs.
Frederickson. Will one of them tell Mrs. Frederickson that
Elena cheated? What will Mrs. Frederickson say? Make up a
dialogue between the teacher and the two students. Act out
your dialogue for the class.

Structure Practice

A. Write the past tense form of each verb. Then use the past
tense forms to complete the sentences. The sentences are not
in order. Be careful.

Verb	Past Tense	Sentence
1. to try	_____	When I _____ up, it was seven o'clock.
2. to wake	_____	They _____ all the answers on the test.
3. to sit	_____	The test _____ at ten o'clock and ended at eleven.
4. to know	_____	Elena _____ to study, but she fell asleep.
5. to begin	_____	Evan _____ in the chair next to Elena.

B. Unscramble the words to make questions. Then write a negative answer to each question. Don't forget to capitalize and punctuate.

Example: you / lunch / did / eat
<u>Did you eat lunch?</u>
<u>No, I didn't eat lunch.</u>

1. the / elena / did / copy / questions
2. do / did / the / all / you / exercises / of
3. we / homework / did / finish / our
4. you / for / did / your / test / study
5. questions / the / know / did / students / many

C. Look at the words below. Which words are count nouns? Which words are mass nouns? Put them in the correct lists. Then choose five words and use them in sentences with <u>much</u> or <u>many</u>.

rice	pencils	questions	chairs	sand
time	money	dollars	answers	salt

Count Nouns (many)   **Mass Nouns** (much)

Stamp of Approval

Before You Read

A. What do you think of when you see the word <u>vacation</u>? Write some words in the map.

Now write three sentences about vacations using the ideas from your map.

B. Look at the picture on page 52. Answer the questions.

1. What is the man doing?
2. What is the woman doing?
3. Where are the man and woman? How can you tell?

C. Do you know what these words mean? Talk about their meanings with a partner. Then use a dictionary to check your work.

across	pocket
beautiful	to point
to enjoy	to shrug one's shoulders
funny look	store
icy	while

D. Use the words in activity C to complete these sentences. Change the form of a word if necessary.

1. Ed _____ the warm sun. He liked it very much.

2. I keep some money, a tissue, and my keys in the

   _____ of my pants.

3. When the water is very cold, it is _____.

4. You can buy needles, thread, and cloth in a sewing

   _____.

5. The beaches in Puerto Rico are _____.

6. The sewing store was _____ the street from

   the hotel.

7. The lady showed Ed the pockets on her dress. She

   _____ to them.

8. Ed listened to music _____ he wrote letters.

9. The man gave Ed a _____ because he didn't

   understand what Ed wanted. He thought Ed was a

   little crazy.

10. People often say "I don't know" and _____ when

    they don't know an answer.

Stamp of Approval

Ed Taylor decided to go to Puerto Rico for vacation. He enjoyed the warm sun, the beautiful beaches, and icy blue water, but he had one problem. He couldn't speak any Spanish. Sometimes he found people who understood him, but sometimes he wasn't so lucky.

Ed liked to sit on the beach and write letters while he listened to music on the radio. He wrote many letters, and then he decided to find the post office and buy some stamps.

Ed walked up to the first person he saw and asked:

"Where can I buy some *bollos,* please?"

The man gave him a funny look and walked away.

Again Ed stopped someone and asked:

"Where can I buy some *sillies,* please?"

The woman shrugged her shoulders and continued walking.
Ed tried again:

"Excuse me, sir, where can I buy some *bolsillos?*"

The man pointed to a little sewing store across the street. Ed
thought it was strange to find stamps in a sewing store, but Ed
thanked the man and went into the store.

"May I please have some *bolsillos* for my letters?"

The lady in the store looked at the letters and then at Ed.

"*Bolsillos?*"

"Yes, to put right here."

And he pointed to the place where the stamp goes.

The lady in the store began to laugh. Ed didn't understand, and
he felt a little annoyed.

"What's so funny?" he asked angrily. "I asked for some
bolsillos for my letters."

Still laughing, the lady pointed to her pockets. "*Estos son
bolsillos.* These are pockets," she said. "You want *sellos*. You can
buy them at the post office, but I think you should buy a dictionary
first."

While You Read

A. As you read, take notes and fill in the chart.

main character	
where he went	
what he did	
what he needed	
what problem he had	
what happened	

Now use your notes to write a summary of the story.

B. Read the story again. Underline each new word you find. Then rewrite the sentences using a synonym or a group of words in place of the underlined words.

After You Read

Comprehension Check

A. Choose the best answer for each question.

1. What did Ed like?
   a. He liked cold weather.
   b. He didn't like to swim.
   c. He enjoyed the beach.

2. What kind of person was Ed?
   a. He was a timid person.
   b. He was a person who kept trying.
   c. He was a smart person.

3. Why did Ed ask for pockets?
   a. He had a hole in his pocket.
   b. He forgot what he wanted to buy.
   c. He didn't know the Spanish word for stamp.

4. What was the lady's reaction?
   a. She got angry.
   b. She laughed.
   c. She began to cry.

5. What advice did the lady give to Ed?
   a. Buy a dictionary.
   b. Buy stamps at the post office.
   c. both (a) and (b)

B. Number these sentences so they tell the story about Ed Taylor. Then check your work with a partner.

_____ He liked to sit on the beach and write letters.

_____ He wanted to buy some stamps, but he didn't know the Spanish word for stamp.

_____ Ed went to Puerto Rico for vacation.

_____ He asked for pockets instead of stamps.

_____ The man he asked sent him to a sewing store.

C. Talk or write about these questions.

1. What words describe Ed Taylor?
2. What do you think Ed Taylor will do when he leaves the sewing shop? Explain your answer.
3. What advice would you give to Ed Taylor before he goes on his next vacation?

Structure Practice

A. Complete each sentence with the correct preposition.

into   of   around   about   up   for

1. He walked _____ the corner.

2. She pressed the elevator button and went _____ to the fourth floor.

3. We spend a lot _____ time studying _____ our tests.

4. It's not nice to talk _____ people behind their backs.

5. Go _____ the store and buy some stamps.

B. Use <u>may</u>, <u>can</u>, or <u>must</u> to complete each sentence. <u>May</u> is for permission, <u>can</u> is for possibility, and <u>must</u> is for obligation.

1. _____ I please have some stamps? (permission)

2. You _____ buy them at the post office. (possibility)

3. Ed _____ buy a good dictionary. (obligation)

4. Why _____ I listen to you? (obligation)

5. _____ I leave the room, please? (permission)

C. Write the past tense form of each verb. Then write a sentence in the past tense for each verb.

Verb	**Past Tense Form**
1. to have	1. _____
2. to find	2. _____
3. to buy	3. _____
4. to give	4. _____
5. to think	5. _____

Sentence

1. _____

2. _____

3. _____

4. _____

5. _____

Story 9

Where's the Hitch?

Before You Read

A. What do you think of when you see the word <u>hitchhike</u>? Write some words in the map.

Now write three sentences about hitchhiking using the ideas from your map.

B. Look at the picture on page 59. Answer the questions.

1. What is the man doing?
2. What are the two girls doing?

C. Read these sentences with a partner. Can you guess the meanings of the underlined words? Use a dictionary if you need help.

Definitions

1. The old man offered the girls money. He was very <u>generous</u>. _____

2. We had ten dollars, but we spent eight. We only have two dollars <u>left</u>. _____

Definitions

3. The girls decided to hitchhike. They waited by the road for someone to give them a ride.   _____

4. Let's hitchhike instead of taking the train. It's cheaper.   _____

5. The old man was good to the girls. They thanked him for his kindness.   _____

6. The girls refused the money the old man offered them. They said, "No, thank you."   _____

7. Don't spend all your money now. Save some for a rainy day, when you really need it.   _____

8. I bought a souvenir for my mother. It was a bracelet from Germany.   _____

9. Brenda and Sheila were spending the summer in Germany.   _____

10. "This man can't speak English. How can we talk to him?" the girls wondered.   _____

D. Match each word or phrase with its meaning. Use a dictionary if you need help.

1. kindness   a. in place of
2. left   b. to say no
3. instead of   c. remaining
4. to wonder   d. goodness
5. to refuse   e. to ask oneself

Where's the Hitch?

Brenda and Sheila were spending their summer in Germany. While they were there, they went on many tours, bought many souvenirs, and spent too much money.

One day, after counting their money, they realized they didn't have much left. They were going to take the train from Munich to Frankfurt, but they wanted to save their money for a rainy day.

"I have an idea," said Brenda. "We were going to take the train, but let's hitchhike instead."

"All right," replied Sheila, "but we must be careful."

The girls were lucky. A kindly old man, who was wearing a white suit and a blue beret, stopped to pick them up. He was driving an old, old car. He was going to Frankfurt, and so the girls got in.

"Do you speak English?" the girls asked.

"*Nein*," the old man said sadly in German.

"How can we speak with him?" the girls wondered. Finally Sheila had an idea.

"We can draw pictures and act out ideas," Sheila said. That is just what they did.

They exchanged stories about their countries and families. The old man explained that it was dangerous to hitchhike. When they arrived in Frankfurt, the old man wanted to give the girls money.

They were surprised and happy. Of course, they refused and asked him why he was so generous. He explained that if they were hitchhiking, they must be poor and in need of money. He wanted to help them.

Brenda and Sheila thanked him very much for his kindness and told him that they were not very poor. They just had to be careful not to spend all the money that they took with them.

While You Read

A. Find these sentences in the story.

1. Write the sentences that tell what Brenda and Sheila were doing in Germany.
2. Write the sentence that tells who gave the girls a ride.
3. Write the sentences that tell how the girls communicated with the old man.
4. Write the sentences that tell why the old man wanted to give the girls money.

B. 1. Complete this time line to show the order of the events in the story.

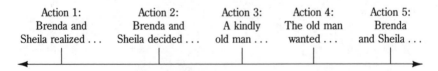

Action 1: Brenda and Sheila realized . . .	Action 2: Brenda and Sheila decided . . .	Action 3: A kindly old man . . .	Action 4: The old man wanted . . .	Action 5: Brenda and Sheila . . .

2. Share your time line with a partner. Then take turns telling the story about Brenda and Sheila. Use your time lines for help.

After You Read

Comprehension Check

A. Choose the best word to complete each sentence.

1. Brenda and Sheila were spending the summer in

    _____.

    a. Italy   b. Australia   c. Germany

2. A/an _____ man gave them a ride.
   a. poor   b. old   c. sad

3. He asked them, "Do you _____ money?"
   a. need   b. like   c. spend

4. The girls thought he was very _____.
   a. dangerous   b. generous   c. surprised

5. Brenda and Sheila were saving their money for a

    _____ day.
    a. poor   b. careful   c. rainy

B. Think about the story. Write words in this chart that help you remember the story. If you need help, look at the story.

place	
characters	
action	
ending	

Use your notes to help you write a summary of the story.

C. 1. You are Sheila. Write a letter to your mother. Tell her about your trip from Munich to Frankfurt.
   2. Exchange letters with a partner. Then pretend you are Sheila's mother. Answer your partner's letter.

Structure Practice

A. Look at the example and then finish each infinitive phrase.

Example: Brenda and Sheila were going to _____ .
Brenda and Sheila were going to <u>take the train.</u>

1. Brenda and Sheila decided to _____ .

2. A man in a blue beret stopped to _____ .

3. The girls wanted to _____ .

4. The old man wanted to _____ .

5. Brenda and Sheila were careful to _____ .

B. Answer the questions in complete sentences.

1. What were Brenda and Sheila doing in Germany?
2. Where were they going?
3. Why were the girls hitchhiking?
4. What was the old man wearing?
5. What was he driving?

C. Write the correct object pronoun next to each subject pronoun.

I _____   it _____

you _____   we _____

he _____   you _____

she _____   they _____

me   him   it   you   her   us   them   you

Now complete the sentences using the correct object pronouns.

1. The old man was nice to the girls.

   He was nice to _____.

2. The girls wanted to speak to the man.

   They wanted to speak to _____.

3. They asked their girlfriend a question.

   They asked _____ a question.

4. The man spoke to Marilyn and me.

   He spoke to _____.

5. I spoke to Lena and you.

   I spoke to _____.

Mismatch

Before You Read

A. What do you think of when you see the phrase <u>blind date</u>? Write some words in the map.

Now write a short paragraph about blind dates using the ideas from your map.

B. Look at the picture on page 66. Answer the questions.

1. What do you see in the picture?
2. What do you think the people in the picture feel? Why?

C. Match each word or phrase with its meaning. Use a dictionary if you need help.

1. to go steady
2. blind date
3. mismatch
4. relationship
5. awkward

  a. connection with another person
  b. embarrassing
  c. to date only one person
  d. a social meeting between two people who have not met before
  e. two things that don't fit together

D. Read the story. Write the words you don't know. Then work with a partner to guess the meanings of the words. Use the story for help. Use a dictionary to check your work.

Words	Definitions
_____	_____
_____	_____
_____	_____
_____	_____
_____	_____
_____	_____
_____	_____
_____	_____
_____	_____

Mismatch

1

Peter and Rhoda were going steady for two years. Everyone thought they were going to get married. One evening while they were eating in a restaurant, Peter said to Rhoda:

"You know, Rhoda, you're the only girl I really know well. We are both very young, and I think we must try to make new friends and have new experiences. If we still love each other after all that, then we can get married."

"That's true, isn't it? But I don't want to stop our relationship, do you? We can see each other, can't we?"

"No, Rhoda, not for a while."

"I guess you're right, but I'm going to miss you very much."

"I'm going to miss you, too, Rhoda."

2

The months passed. Rhoda and Peter were very lonely. It was hard to meet someone they really liked. They were always going to different places, meeting different friends, doing different things, but they were still not happy.

Rhoda finally decided to try a computer dating service. She filled out an application which told what she liked in a person, what her hobbies were, and what kind of person she wanted to meet.

3

Rhoda was having second thoughts about the dating service, when the phone rang. It was Andre LeGros who received her name from the computer service. They arranged to meet that evening for coffee. While she was waiting for Andre, Peter came in. She asked him:

"What are you doing here?"

"Well, I have a blind date for tonight with a girl named April May. It's a computer match, so she must be the girl of my dreams. What are you doing here?"

"I'm waiting for my blind date. His name is Andre LeGros."

4

After a few minutes of awkward silence, Rhoda began to laugh. She said:

"I'm April May."

Peter looked surprised. After a moment, he said:

"And I'm Andre LeGros. This was no mismatch, was it? It was meant to be."

While You Read

A. While you read, complete this chart. Put an X in the "yes" or "no" column for each person.

	Peter		Rhoda	
	yes	no	yes	no
was going steady for two years				
is very young				
knows only one girl well				
feels lonely after they break up				
meets someone he/she really likes				
tries a computer dating service				
has second thoughts about the dating service				
is April May				
is Andre LeGros				

B. Read the story again. Stop after each section to answer the question.

Section 1. Why did Peter and Rhoda stop seeing each other?
Section 2. How did Peter and Rhoda feel?
Section 3. Whom did Rhoda arrange to meet?
Section 4. Who was Rhoda's blind date? Who was Peter's blind date?

After You Read

Comprehension Check

A. One of the choices for each question is wrong. Find the wrong answer and correct it.

1. In the restaurant, Peter said to Rhoda:
   a. "We're both very young."
   b. "I never want to marry you."
   c. "We must try to make new friends."

2. Rhoda said to Peter:
   a. "I don't want to see you anymore."
   b. "I don't want to stop our relationship."
   c. "I'm going to miss you very much."

3. The months passed.
   a. Rhoda and Peter were very lonely.
   b. It was hard to meet someone they really liked.
   c. They never went anywhere.

4. Rhoda tried a computer dating service.
   a. She filled out an application.
   b. She had second thoughts about the dating service.
   c. Peter called her to tell her he loved her.

5. Rhoda arranged to meet her blind date for coffee.
   a. Her blind date couldn't see.
   b. Andre LeGros was really Peter.
   c. Peter had a date with April May.

B. Match column **A** with column **B** to form complete sentences.

A	B
1. Peter and Rhoda were	a. finds you blind dates.
2. Rhoda didn't want	b. going steady for two years.
3. A computer dating service	c. was really Rhoda.
4. Andre LeGros	d. to stop their relationship.
5. April May	e. was really Peter.

C. Finish the story of Rhoda and Peter. Did they get married? Did they leave each other and meet someone new? Were they happy? Did they try another dating service? Share your story with the class.

Structure Practice

A. Finish the sentences. Tell what you are going to do this weekend.

1. I am going to _____.

2. Then I am going to _____.

3. After that I am going to _____.

4. Then maybe I'm going to _____.

5. I am also going to _____.

B. Fill in the blanks with the past continuous tense of each verb. Follow the example.

Example: I <u>was going</u> to school.
         (to go)

I met Peter last year while I _____ in the library.
         (to study)

We fell in love. Everyone _____ me what to do. I
                               (to tell)

_____ because I was confused and I _____ to
  (to cry)   (to listen)

everyone. Finally Peter said he _____ me a wedding
                                    (to buy)

ring. I was happy, but I decided to finish school before I

got married.

C. Add a tag question to each sentence. Follow the example.

Example: She likes you, <u>doesn't she?</u>
She doesn't like you, <u>does she?</u>

1. You hear me, _____?

   You don't hear me, _____?

2. They are going steady, _____?

   They aren't going steady, _____?

3. Rhoda is sad, _____?

   Rhoda isn't sad, _____?

4. You are my blind date, _____?

   You aren't my blind date, _____?

5. We want to be together, _____?

   We don't want to be together, _____?

The Picture of Confusion

Before You Read

A. What do you think of when you see the word <u>museum</u>? Write some words in the map.

museum

Now write a short paragraph about museums using the ideas from your map.

B. Look at the picture on page 73. Answer the questions.

1. What do you see in the picture?
2. Why do you think the boy is crying?
3. What do you think will happen next?

C. Read the story. Write the words you don't know. Then work with a partner to guess the meanings of the words. Use the story for help. Use a dictionary to check your work.

Words	**Definitions**
_____	_____
_____	_____
_____	_____
_____	_____
_____	_____
_____	_____
_____	_____
_____	_____
_____	_____

D. Choose the correct synonym for each word or phrase.

1. curator
   a. bandage   b. caretaker   c. cured

2. to make the rounds
   a. to draw circles   b. to dance   c. to inspect

3. to have deep meaning
   a. to have a lot   b. to say a lot   c. to say a little
      of water

4. such a painting
   a. the opposite of   b. not like that   c. a painting
                                                 like that

5. to review
   a. to describe   b. to see again   c. to speak
      and criticize

The Picture of Confusion

It was six o'clock in the evening. No one was left in the museum. José Menendez, the curator, was making the rounds, checking to see that everything was all right. Suddenly, José saw something on the floor. He walked over to see what it was. What do you think he saw? He saw a beautiful abstract painting lying there. José showed the painting to the director of the museum. The director asked him a couple of questions.

"Where did you find this?"

"On the floor, on the fourth floor," answered José.

"Who painted it?"

"I don't know. There's no name."

"Let's call several museums to check and see if it's a stolen painting," said the director.

No one claimed the painting, so the director decided to hang it in the abstract art division of the museum. All the experts came to review the painting. Each one said it was beautiful and had very deep meaning. The director was proud to have such a painting in his museum. He congratulated José on his discovery.

Several weeks later, a woman came to the museum with her five-year-old son. While they were looking at the new painting, the little boy began to cry bitterly. The director came over to the child and asked:

"Why are you crying?"

The child pointed to the painting and said:

"I'm crying because that's my painting on the wall, and I want it back."

"Yes," said his mother, "I was here with Danny a few weeks ago, and he left his painting right here on the floor. If you look carefully, you can see his name."

The director was embarrassed. He looked at the boy and his mother awkwardly. He did not know what to say.

While You Read

A. As you read, take notes and fill in the chart.

what the story is about	
who found it	
where he found it	
what he did with it	
what happened to it	
who claimed it	

Now use your notes to tell the story to a partner. Listen while your partner tells the story to you.

B. Think about these questions while you read. Then answer the questions.

1. What kind of museum is this?
2. Why did the curator show the painting to the director?
3. What do you think abstract art is?
4. Do you like abstract art? Why or why not?
5. Do you think a child's painting can fool experts?
6. What makes a person an expert? Are experts always right?

After You Read

Comprehension Check

A. Write **T** if the sentence is true. Write **F** if it is false. If a sentence is false, change it to make it true.

1. José Menendez, the director, was making the rounds.
2. José saw a beautiful abstract painting on the floor.
3. The experts said the painting had very little meaning.
4. A little boy began to laugh when he saw the painting.
5. The boy didn't want the painting.

B. Choose the best answer for each question.

1. Where did José find the painting?
   a. at six o'clock in the evening
   b. on the floor, on the fourth floor
   c. in the abstract art division

2. What did the museum director do?
   a. He claimed the painting.
   b. He found the painting.
   c. He checked to see if it was a stolen painting.

3. Who reviewed the painting?
   a. all the experts
   b. a five-year-old boy
   c. José Menendez, the curator

4. Why did the boy begin to cry?
   a. He didn't like the painting
   b. He didn't see the painting.
   c. He wanted his painting back.

5. What was on the painting?
   a. the boy's name
   b. the mother's name
   c. the curator's name

C. What will the museum director say to the boy and his mother? What will he do with the painting? Talk about the problem in groups of three. Then role-play the conversation between the museum director, the boy, and his mother.

Structure Practice

A. Write a sentence that tells about something. Then write a sentence that compares two things. Follow the examples.

Examples: a. interesting—more interesting
That painting is <u>interesting</u>.
This painting is <u>more interesting</u> than that one.

   b. easy—easier
That story is <u>easy</u> to understand.
This story is <u>easier</u> to understand than that one.

1. big—bigger
   That room is big.
   This room is _____ than that one.

2. beautiful—more beautiful

3. bright—brighter

4. complicated—more complicated

5. pretty—prettier

6. expensive—more expensive

B. Answer the questions in complete sentences.

1. Which is the biggest museum?

Bigtown   **Centerville**   **Metropolis**

2. Which is the biggest painting?

Joe's   **Mike's**   **Shelley's**

3. Which is the most expensive painting?

$45.00   **$25.00**   **$150.00**
Elena's   **Seth's**   **Peter's**

C. Write a sentence for each picture. Follow the examples.
Examples:

a. (as happy as)   **Alain**   **Un Hee**

Alain isn't <u>as happy as</u> Un Hee.

b. (as big as)   **Jeff**   **Craig**

Jeff is <u>as big as</u> Craig.

1. (as beautiful as)   **Bob's painting**   **Harry's painting**

2. (as interesting as)   **The Museum**   **The Museum of**
                          of Art   **Natural History**

3. (as expensive as)   **crayons**   **markers**

4. (as old as)   **Jennifer**   **Robin**

5. (as happy as)   **Leo**   **Michele**

Story 12

All Keyed Up

Before You Read

A. What do you think of when you see the word <u>key</u>? Write some words in the map.

Now write four sentences about keys using the ideas from your map.

B. Look at the picture on page 82. Answer the questions.

1. What do you see in the picture?
2. What do you think the people in the picture will say to each other?

C. Do you know what these words mean? Talk about their meanings with a partner. Then use a dictionary to check your work.

alarm system	identification
camping	to keep an eye on
exhausted	keyed up
frightened	promptly
to guess	set

D. Use the words in activity C to complete these sentences. Change the form of a word if necessary.

1. Gail and Howard went _____ for two weeks. They slept in a tent.

2. Gail and Howard were very tired and they wanted to sleep. They were _____.

3. A birth certificate and a driver's license are two useful pieces of _____.

4. I have a _____ of three keys for the house and a key for the car.

5. I _____ we must find a way to get inside. We can't stay out here.

6. Don't get all _____! Just calm down and try to relax.

7. Someone has to watch the suitcases. I'll _____ them while you look for the keys.

8. An _____ makes noise to warn people of danger.

9. The neighbor was _____ by the noise. She thought a robber was in the house.

10. The police arrived _____. They came right away.

All Keyed Up

Gail and Howard liked to travel. Every vacation they went to a different place. They were always careful when they left the house. They locked the doors and windows and put on the alarm system. Then Gail took the extra set of keys and left them with her mother.

Gail and Howard spent two weeks camping in the mountains.
They had a great time, but when they came home, all they wanted
to do was sleep.

"Give me the keys, Howie. Let me open the door while you
park the car."

"Uh, oh, Gail. I can't find the keys. You have them, don't you?"

"No, Howie. I gave them to you. Look again."

"Really, Gail. I don't have them."

They both looked everywhere, but no luck. The keys were not
anywhere.

"Don't get all keyed up. Go to your mom's house, Gail, and get
the extra set. Let me keep an eye on the suitcases."

Gail went to her mother's house, but her mother wasn't home.

"Well, Howie, I guess we must find a way to get inside."

Howard climbed up the fire escape to open a window, but he forgot that the window was locked, too. He climbed back down, found a metal bar, broke the window, and climbed into the house. He went to open the front door for Gail, only to find the police.

A frightened neighbor heard the noise and thought there was a robbery; so she called the police. Howard was almost arrested, but luckily he had identification that proved that he lived in that house.

Finally, both exhausted, Gail and Howard brought their luggage in, climbed into bed, and promptly fell asleep.

While You Read

A. As you read, take notes and fill in the chart.

What Gail and Howard did . . .

before their vacation	
on their vacation	
when they got home	
when the police came	
when they got inside	

Now use your notes to write a summary of the story.

B. Read the story again. Underline each new word you find. Then rewrite the sentences using a synonym or a group of words in place of the underlined words.

After You Read

Comprehension Check

A. Write **T** if the sentence is true and **F** if the sentence is false. Correct the sentence if it is false.

1. Gail and Howard were always careful when they left the house.
2. They took a plane to Japan.
3. When they came home, they couldn't find their keys.
4. Howard broke down the door.
5. He was arrested.

B. Find the questions that are answered in the story. Answer them first. Then make up your own answers to the other questions. Share your answers with a partner.

1. What did Gail and Howard do on their vacation?
2. Where are Gail and Howard's keys?
3. Where is Gail's mother?
4. How did Howard get into the house?
5. Who called the police?

C. In groups of three, role-play the conversation between Gail, Howard, and the police officer.

Structure Practice

A. Match the infinitives in column A with their past tense forms in column B.

A	B
1. to like	a. were/was
2. to go	b. spent
3. to be	c. took
4. to leave	d. wanted
5. to put	e. left
6. to lock	f. forgot
7. to take	g. thought
8. to spend	h. liked
9. to have	i. heard
10. to come	j. came
11. to want	k. went
12. to forget	l. locked
13. to find	m. found
14. to hear	n. had
15. to think	o. put

B. Complete the questions using <u>do</u>, <u>does</u>, or <u>did</u>.

1. _____ you forget the keys to the house yesterday?

2. _____ she want to go to her mother's house now?

3. _____ Howard feel very tired yesterday?

4. _____ we have to go home now?

5. _____ the dog want to eat now?

C. Change these yes/no questions to information questions.

1. Are you going home now? (Where)
2. Was he eating chicken and rice for supper? (What)
3. Am I leaving at one o'clock? (When)
4. Were you walking to school with John? (Who)
5. Is he feeling well today? (How)

Grand Delusions

Before You Read

A. What do you think of when you see the word <u>family</u>? Write some words in the map.

Now write four sentences about families using the ideas from your map.

B. Look at the picture on page 88. Answer the questions.

1. What do you see in the picture?
2. Would you like to be in this place? Why or why not?

C. Read these sentences with a partner. Can you guess the meanings of the underlined words and phrases? Use a dictionary if you need help.

Definitions

1. Andy didn't want to get a dog, but he got one <u>anyway</u>. _____

Definitions

2. A guidance <u>counselor</u> helps
    students plan their
    schedules.   _____

3. When a place is <u>crowded</u>, it
    has too many things or
    people.   _____

4. My house is too crowded. I
    <u>can't stand</u> it anymore.   _____

5. Your house is <u>roomier</u> than
    mine. It's not as crowded.   _____

6. Andy spoke to Mr. Chong
    on Monday. The <u>next</u> day
    was Tuesday.   _____

7. A guidance counselor helps
    students <u>solve</u> their
    problems.   _____

8. Mr. Chong had a <u>crazy</u> idea.
    It didn't seem sensible.   _____

9. Andy <u>threatened</u> to move
    into the school. He warned
    Mr. Chong about what he
    would do.   _____

10. A <u>wise</u> person knows many
    things.   _____

D. Write **T** if the sentence is true and **F** if it is false. Correct the
sentence if it is false.

1. A crowded room is empty.
2. When you can't stand something, you are happy with it.
3. A wise person is very intelligent.
4. If you take out the table, the kitchen will be roomier.
5. When you solve a problem, you cannot find an answer.

Grand Delusions

Andy is learning about the family.

"How many people live in your house?" asks Mrs. Hill, Andy's teacher.

"My house is very crowded," answers Andy. "I live with my parents, four brothers, and two sisters. I can't stand it anymore. I can't find a place to do my work."

"Why don't you speak to your counselor?" asks Mrs. Hill.

The next day, Andy made an appointment with Mr. Chong.

"Sure, there's a way to solve your problem. Get a dog," advised Mr. Chong.

"The man is crazy. Living in a crowded house can't be one of his problems," thought Andy.

But Andy got a dog anyway. The next day, he went to see his counselor and told him it was much too crowded.

"Ask your aunts, uncles, and their children to stay for a while, and oh, yes, get a cat."

"You're a counselor, and you must know. But that sounds crazy to me," said Andy.

The next day, Andy complained bitterly to Mr. Chong.

"I can't stand it anymore. I sleep in the hall."

"Well, ask some friends to stay for a few days."

"This guy is mad!" cried Andy.

But he invited his friends anyway. Every inch of the house was occupied. When Andy threatened to move into the school, Mr. Chong told him to send his friends home. The next day, Andy went to Mr. Chong's office and said:

"Oh, there's much more room now. I can breathe a little."

Next, Mr. Chong told him to send his relatives home.

"Oh, Mr. Chong, you're very wise. I have so much room. I don't know where to put myself," said Andy.

"Now, Andy, sell your dog and your cat."

Andy returned the following day and thanked Mr. Chong for telling him how to make his house roomier.

"I wonder how he did it?" Andy asked himself. "Here I am with parents, four brothers, and two sisters; yet the house seems so much bigger than before."

While You Read

A. As you read, take notes and fill in the chart.

Andy's problem	
Mrs. Hill's suggestion	
Mr. Chong's first suggestion	
Mr. Chong's second suggestion	
Mr. Chong's third suggestion	
Mr. Chong's fourth suggestion	
Mr. Chong's fifth suggestion	
Mr. Chong's last suggestion	
the result	

Use your notes to help you tell the story to a partner. Listen while your partner tells you the story.

B.   Find these sentences in the story.

1. Write the sentences that tell what problem Andy has.
2. Write three sentences that tell what Andy thinks about Mr. Chong.
3. Write the sentence that tells the first suggestion Mr. Chong made.
4. Write the sentence that tells the last suggestion Mr. Chong made.
5. Write the sentence that tells how Andy felt at the end of the story.

After You Read

Comprehension Check

A. Number these sentences so they tell the story about Andy.
Then check your work with a partner.

_____ Mr. Chong told him to get a dog and a cat, and
to invite his family and friends.

_____ Andy's house was very crowded.

_____ Then Mr. Chong told him to sell the cat and dog
and to send everyone home.

_____ He made an appointment with his guidance
counselor, Mr. Chong.

_____ The house seemed much bigger to Andy.

B. Complete the sentences. Write the words in the boxes at the
right. Then unscramble the circled letters to find the word that
will complete the bonus sentence.

1. Andy's house was
   too _____.

2. Mr. Chong told
   Andy to invite
   his
   _____.

3. Andy thought Mr. Chong was
   _____.

4. Then Mr. Chong told Andy to
_____ his relatives home.

5. Then Andy thought Mr. Chong was
very _____.

Bonus: Andy was happy he _____ to Mr. Chong.

C. What do you think about Mr. Chong's advice? Talk to a
partner. What different advice could you give Andy? Make up
a conversation between Andy and another guidance counselor,
Mrs. Wujek. Act out your conversation for the class.

Structure Practice

A. Match the subject pronouns in column A with the possessive
pronouns in column B.

A	B
1. I	a. her, hers
2. you	b. our, ours
3. he	c. your, yours
4. she	d. it, its
5. it	e. their, theirs
6. we	f. my, mine
7. you	g. his, his
8. they	h. your, yours

Now write two sentences for each picture. Follow the example.

Example: This is my book.
This is <u>mine</u>.

1.   a. _____ (his)

b. _____ (his)

2. a. _____ (her)

b. _____ (hers)

3. a. _____ (my)

b. _____ (mine)

4. a. _____ (their)

b. _____ (theirs)

5. a. _____ (our)

b. _____ (ours)

B. Use 's to make a possessive noun. Then write a sentence using the possessive form.

Example: Maria   Maria's test was difficult.
            test

1. Susan   _____
   hair

2. My teacher _____
   book

3. The child   _____
   dog

4. The student _____
   grades

5. Jack   _____
   bicycle

C. Complete the sentences with <u>can</u>, <u>may</u>, or <u>must</u>. Can is for possibility; may is for permission; and must is for obligation.

1. My house is too crowded. I _____ have more room.

2. _____ you please help me?

3. _____ I ask you a question?

4. I _____ not find a place to do my work.

5. He doesn't feel well. He _____ stay home today.

Story 14

A Communication Problem

Before You Read

A. What do you think of when you see the word <u>train</u>? Write some words in the map.

Now write a short paragraph about trains using the ideas from your map.

B. Look at the picture on page 97. Answer the questions.

1. What do you see in the picture?
2. Who do you think is talking?

C. Do you know what these words and phrases mean? Talk about their meanings with a partner. Then use a dictionary to check your work.

as a result	to receive
to miss	satisfied
out of order	to sit back
to pull into	transportation authority
rear	usually

95

D. Use the words in activity C to complete these sentences. Change the form of a word if necessary.

1. I like to _____ in that comfortable chair and read a good book.

2. The train _____ the station right on time.

3. It is _____ hot in the summer.

4. We'll have to take the stairs. The elevator is _____.

5. You sent me a letter on Monday. I _____ it on Wednesday.

6. The _____ raised the bus fare from a dollar to a dollar and twenty-five cents.

7. I _____ my train. I got to the station five minutes after it left.

8. Some people like to sit at the front of the train, but I like to sit at the _____.

9. We didn't hear the conductor announce our stop.

   _____, we didn't get off.

10. I got a 95 on my English test. I was _____ with my grade.

A Communication Problem

1   Train number 814 used to go from New York to Philadelphia and back four times every day. Number 814 used to be full of people who were traveling for business. They usually enjoyed the ride. However, in June of 1979, the transportation authority began to receive many letters of complaint.

2 "We like to ride at the back of the train each time we take a trip," wrote many passengers. "And we can't hear the conductor when he announces the stops. The loudspeaker that used to announce the stops is out of order. As a result, we often miss our stops. Please help us."

3 After many hours of careful thought, the people at the transportation authority decided to put a conductor at the back of the train to announce the stops. They wanted all their passengers to be satisfied.

4 Soon there were two conductors to announce the stops on train number 814. The passengers sat back, relaxed, and waited to hear the conductors announce their stops. As the train pulled into the first stop, the conductor at the head of the train called out:

"Newark here, Newark, New Jersey!"

The conductor at the rear of the train called out:

"Here too, here too."

While You Read

A. Keep a mini-literature log. After you read each section of the story, write a sentence that tells your reaction. Follow one of these examples or make up your own "I" sentences:

> I wonder why...
> I like the way...
> I want to know...
> I'm surprised that ...
> If I were ...

B. Read the story again. Stop after each section to answer the questions.

Section 1. Where did train number 814 go? How often did it run?

Section 2. What problem did the passengers have?

Section 3. How did the transportation authority plan to solve the problem?

Section 4. Did the solution work? Why or why not?

After You Read

Comprehension Check

A. Choose the answer that best completes each sentence.

1. The train number was
   a. eighteen fourteen.
   b. eight hundred fourteen.
   c. eight hundred forty.

2. The transportation authority received complaints because
   a. the train was broken.
   b. the passengers were deaf.
   c. the loudspeaker was broken.

3. The transportation authority decided to
   a. fix the loudspeaker.
   b. put a conductor at the back of each train.
   c. ignore the complaints.

4. The people at the transportation authority wanted the passengers to be
   a. upset.   b. happy.   c. nervous.

5. The conductor at the rear of the train was
   a. stupid.   b. sleeping.   c. forgetful.

B. Look at the first three paragraphs in the story. What is the main idea of each paragraph? What or whom does each paragraph talk about?

	Main Idea	**Subject**
Paragraph 1	_____	_____
Paragraph 2	_____	_____
Paragraph 3	_____	_____

Share your answers with a partner.

C. What do you think will happen next? Write a short paragraph that tells what the passengers, the conductors, and the transportation authority will do to solve the problem.

Structure Practice

A. Change the underlined verbs to the past tense form with used to + infinitive. Follow the example.

Example: I walked to school.
I used to walk to school.

Train number 814 went from New York to Philadelphia. It was full of people who traveled for business. They enjoyed the ride. However, the people who rode in the back of the train complained about the conductor. They couldn't hear him.

B. These words are homonyms. They sound the same but are spelled differently. They also have different meanings. Write a sentence for each meaning.

1. to
   two
   too
2. hear
   here
3. for
   fore
   four
4. we
   wee
   whee

5. our
   hour
6. all
   awl
7. they're
   their
   there
8. be
   bee

C. Complete the sentences with the correct prepositions. Some of the prepositions are used more than once.

for   from   in   at   to   on   up   around   about   of

1. May I please have a box _____ cookies?

2. I live far away _____ the school.

3. I have a letter _____ you _____ Mary.

4. He lives _____ Kansas.

5. We live _____ John Street _____ number 110.

6. Don't talk _____ me behind my back.

7. Please pick _____ the papers _____ the floor.

8. Walk _____ the corner and see if John is there.

9. My aunt came _____ my house to visit yesterday.

10. My school is _____ Maple Street.

Story 15

Inside Out

Before You Read

A. What do you think of when you see the word <u>shopping</u>? Write some words in the map.

Now write a short paragraph about shopping using the ideas from your map.

B. Look at the picture on page 103. Answer the questions.

1. What do you see in the picture?
2. What is the girl outside the building doing?
3. What is the girl inside the building doing?
4. What do you think this story will be about?

C. Look for these words and phrases and underline them in the story. Then write a definition for each one. Use the story for help.

around the corner	lobby
block	to make an appointment
by herself/himself	on time
classmates	over a/an _____
inside out	to show up

Compare definitions with a partner. Use a dictionary to check the meaning of any word or phrase you disagree about.

D. Complete each sentence with a word or phrase from the list in activity C. Change the form of a word if necessary.

1. I waited for an hour, but he never _____.

2. Maryse didn't come, so Sheila left _____.

3. I _____ to see the dentist at 9:00 A.M.

4. I waited for _____ hour, and then I left.

5. I live at 539 Cherry Street. Steve's house is _____, on Park Avenue.

Inside Out

Sheila wanted to buy a new dress. She didn't want to go shopping by herself, so she called her friend Maryse. They arranged to meet at 100 Frank Street and to spend the day shopping.

Sheila waited for over an hour in front of 100 Frank Street, but Maryse didn't come. She walked up and down the block, across the street, but still Maryse didn't show up. Sheila knew Maryse usually came late, but one hour late was just too much.

Luckily, there was a telephone on the corner.

"I'll call Maryse and see if she's still at home," said Sheila to herself.

"Hello," said a voice.

"Hi, this is Sheila. Is Maryse there?"

"No, she left awhile ago. Look again, maybe she is there now."

"All right. Thank you. Goodbye."

Sheila looked again and then left by herself.

"When will Maryse learn to be on time?" wondered Sheila.

While she was shopping, Sheila met some classmates and told them never to make an appointment with Maryse.

"I'll be her friend," said Sheila, "but I'll never make another date with her."

That night, she called Maryse.

"Where were you? I waited for over an hour for you! I'll never make another appointment with you again."

"What do you mean, Sheila? I'm the one who will never make an appointment with you again. I waited almost two hours for you."

"How can that be? I walked around the corner, up and down the block, across the street, and I didn't see you."

"Of course not, Sheila, you didn't look inside. It was hot, so I went in and sat down in the lobby. I walked out to look for you, but you were probably looking for me around the corner."

Next time, let's decide to meet either inside or outside, not just 'at' the place. I don't want another inside-out day."

While You Read

A. While you read, complete this chart. Put an X in the "yes" or "no" column for each person.

	Sheila		Maryse	
	yes	no	yes	no
wanted to buy a new dress				
is usually late				
called her friend				
was angry				
talked about her friend				
left by herself				
looked outside				
looked inside				
waited outside				
waited inside				

B. 1. Complete this time line to show the order of the events in the story.

Action 1:   Action 2:   Action 3:   Action 4:   Action 5:   Action 6:
Sheila   Sheila   Then   That night   Maryse   Sheila
arranged ...   waited ... Sheila ...   Sheila ...   said ...   said ...

2. Share your time line with a partner. Then take turns telling the story about Sheila and Maryse. Use your time lines for help.

After You Read

Comprehension Check

A. Complete this section of the story. Then check your work with a partner.

Sheila wanted to buy a new _____. She didn't want to

go shopping _____, so she called her friend Maryse.

They _____ to meet at 100 Frank Street and to

_____ the day shopping.

Sheila waited for over an hour _____ 100 Frank

Street, but Maryse didn't come. She walked up and down the

_____, across the street, but still Maryse didn't

_____. Sheila knew Maryse _____ came late, but

one hour late was just too much.

Luckily, there was a _____ on the corner.

"I'll call Maryse and see if she's still _____," said

Sheila to herself.

B. Talk or write about these questions.

1. Why didn't Sheila want to go shopping by herself? Do you like to shop by yourself? Why or why not?
2. Why did Sheila and Maryse arrange to meet at 100 Frank Street?

3. Do you think Sheila and Maryse will ever make another appointment with each other? Why or why not?
4. Who was wrong, Sheila or Maryse? (Was either one wrong?) Why?
5. How long would you wait for a friend to show up?

C. At school the next day, Sheila sees the classmates she talked to about Maryse. What does she say? Role-play the conversation in groups of three.

Structure Practice

A. What will Sheila do? Write complete sentences.

Example: buy / dress   Sheila will buy a dress.

1. wait / bus
2. meet / friend
3. talk / telephone
4. walk / corner
5. take / train

B. Match the subject pronouns in column A with the reflexive pronouns in column B.

1. I	a. yourself
2. you	b. herself
3. he	c. ourselves
4. she	d. themselves
5. it	e. himself
6. we	f. yourselves
7. you	g. myself
8. they	h. itself

Now write sentences with these words. Use the correct reflexive pronoun in each sentence.

Example: Paul / walk / school
       <u>Paul walks to school by himself.</u>

1. You and I / play / chess
2. My sister and you / study
3. You / eat / dinner
4. She / go / school
5. The cat / wash
6. Jim / Peggy / go / movies
7. I / take / bus

C. These prepositions express position. Write a sentence for each preposition.

Example: next to
       <u>John sits next to me in my English class.</u>

1. over
2. under
3. behind
4. in front of
5. in back of
6. inside
7. outside

Which Date Is Which?

Before You Read

A. What do you think of when you see the word <u>date</u>? Write some words in the map.

date

Now write four sentences about dates using the ideas from your map.

B. Look at the picture on page 110. Answer the questions.

1. What do you see in the picture?
2. Why do you think the boys are in the tree?
3. What do you think this story will be about?

C. Match each word or phrase with its definition. Check your work with a partner. Look at the story if you need help.

1. don't worry	a. since
2. cheer up	b. be happy
3. high marks	c. (1) an appointment; (2) a person with whom you have an appointment; (3) a fruit

108

4. delicious	d. to say you will do something
5. as long as	e. timid, bashful
6. date	f. a tropical tree
7. to promise	g. good grades
8. to miss	h. tasty
9. palm tree	i. don't be upset
10. shy	j. to want something you don't have anymore

D. These words are homographs. They are spelled the same, but they have different meanings. Write a definition for each word. Use a dictionary if you need help.

1. date	2. palm	3. miss	4. shy	5. can
date	palm	miss	shy	can

Check your definitions with a partner. Then write five sentences together. Each sentence should use a pair of homographs. Share your sentences with the class.

Which Date Is Which?

Nanou was a new student at Midland High School. She didn't have many friends and was very shy because she didn't speak English well.

"I wish I were back in my native country," thought Nanou. "I used to have many friends; I used to go out a lot; I used to get high marks on every test. Now I have few friends; I never go out; and I just pass. I miss everything: the food, the sunshine, the palm trees, my relatives." After school one day, she met her friend Carol.

"Why are you so sad?" asked Carol.

"In my country, I used to have lots of dates but here I have none."

"I'll get you some, don't worry!" Carol promised. "Cheer up!"

A few days later, Carol showed up with five boys.

"What's all this?" asked Nanou.

"You said you used to have a lot of dates in your country, but here you have none. So I brought you some dates."

Nanou started to laugh and laugh.

"I'm glad to see you're laughing, Nanou, but what's so funny?"

"Carol, I didn't mean boys. I meant the dates that grow on palm trees. They're a delicious fruit. But as long as you brought me these dates, I'll take them, too."

While You Read

A. As you read, take notes and fill in the chart.

main character	
what her life was like before	
what her life is like now	
what she tells Carol	
what Carol does	
what is so funny	

B. Read the story again. Underline each new word you find. Then rewrite the sentences using a synonym or a group of words in place of the underlined words.

After You Read

Comprehension Check

A. Write **T** if the sentence is true and **F** if it is false. Correct the sentence if it is false.

1. Nanou was shy because she was afraid of people.
2. Nanou didn't miss her native country at all.
3. She used to have a lot of dates.
4. Carol brought Nanou some dates.
5. The dates Carol brought grew on palm trees.

B. Complete the sentences.

   1. Nanou felt lonely because . . .
   2. Nanou didn't get high marks because . . .
   3. Carol was a good friend because . . .
   4. Nanou laughed because . . .
   5. Nanou was happy with the dates Carol brought because . . .

C. 1. You are Carol. You want to help Nanou feel happier in her
         new country. What can you do? Make a list of ideas to share
         with the class.
     2. You are Nanou. You want to make more friends and improve
         your English. What can you do? Make a list of ideas to
         share with the class.

Structure Practice

A. **Homonyms** are words that sound the same but are spelled
   differently and have different meanings.

   Homographs are words that sound the same and have the
   same spelling, but have different meanings.

   Read the sentences below. Circle the words that are
   homonyms. Underline the words that are homographs.

   1. "I would give you some food, but I have none," said
      the nun.
   2. The late Mr. Jenkins was always late for his
      appointments.
   3. Did you break the gas pedal or the brake pedal?
   4. Please find some change while I change the tire.
   5. "I'll sell you some bread for a small sum of money," the
      clerk said.

B. Write the simple past, continuous past, and future tenses of each verb. Follow the example.

Infinitive	Simple Past	Past Continuous	Future
Example: to have	had	was having	will have
1. to go	_____	_____	_____
2. to miss	_____	_____	_____
3. to meet	_____	_____	_____
4. to get	_____	_____	_____
5. to say	_____	_____	_____
6. to bring	_____	_____	_____
7. to start	_____	_____	_____
8. to laugh	_____	_____	_____
9. to grow	_____	_____	_____
10. to take	_____	_____	_____

C. Change each sentence to the future tense. Follow the example.

Example: I go to school every day.
I will go to school every day.

1. Henry walks the dog after school.
2. Ramona studies hard for her English tests.
3. Paul plays the piano.
4. Sarah eats pizza with her friends.
5. Steven misses his relatives and friends.

The Perfect Arrangement

Before You Read

A. What do you think of when you see the word <u>anniversary</u>? Write some words in the map.

Now write four sentences about anniversaries using the ideas from your map.

B. Look at the picture on page 116. Answer the questions.

1. What do you see in the picture?
2. Whose anniversary do you think it is?
3. What do you think this story will be about?

C. Read these sentences with a partner. Can you guess the meanings of the underlined words? Use a dictionary if you need help.

Definitions

1. We were married ten years ago. Today is our tenth wedding <u>anniversary.</u>

   _____

2. Sweeping, washing dishes, and washing clothes are household <u>chores.</u>

   _____

Definitions

3. Robbery and murder are
   <u>crimes</u>.   _____

4. English is not difficult if you
   study. Then it's <u>easy</u>.   _____

5. Many people are unemployed
   because of the country's
   <u>economic</u> problems.   _____

6. If there were more police,
   maybe we could <u>eliminate</u>
   crime.   _____

7. I <u>invested</u> my money in oil
   and I <u>invested</u> my time in
   our children.   _____

8. We didn't have much food,
   but we <u>managed</u> to eat a
   little bit every day.   _____

9. I hope we will <u>stay</u> happy
   forever.   _____

10. I have a lot of work <u>to take
    care of</u>. Will you help me?   _____

D. Choose the best word or phrase to complete each sentence.

1. Stella and Joe are celebrating their twenty-fifth wedding

   _____.
   a. eliminate   b. anniversary   c. chores

2. Please _____ the shopping for me.
   a. invest   b. take care of   c. manage

3. This country has many _____ problems.
   a. economic   b. easy   c. chores

4. Don't leave me alone! Please _____ with me.
   a. manage   b. take care of   c. stay

5. The English test will be _____ if you study for it.
   a. easy   b. economic   c. crime

The Perfect Arrangement

Stella and Joe gave a twenty-fifth anniversary party for themselves. After all the years, they were still very happy and loved each other very much. At the party, a friend asked them how they managed to stay happily married through the years. Joe answered:

"That's easy. I take care of the big chores and she takes care of the little ones."

Stella agreed with her husband. She said:

"That's right. I decide where the children should go to school, where we should live, how we should invest our money, and where we should go on vacation. He decides how to keep peace in the world, how to solve the country's economic problems, and how to eliminate crime."

While You Read

A. While you read, complete this chart. Put an X in the "yes" or "no" column for each person.

	Stella		Joe	
	yes	no	yes	no
has been married for 25 years				
decides where the children should go to school				
decides how to eliminate crime				
decides how they should invest their money				
decides where to go on vacation				
decides how to keep peace in the world				
decides how to solve the country's economic problems				
decides where they should live				
is very happy				

B. Read *The Perfect Arrangement* to a partner. Your partner
listens. Read the story again. Your partner fills in the blanks
below. Read the story one more time. Your partner checks his
or her work.

Stella and Joe gave a twenty-fifth _____ party for

themselves. After all the _____, they were still very happy

and _____ each very much. At the _____, a friend

asked them how they _____ to stay happily married through

the _____. Joe answered:

"That's easy. I take _____ of the big chores and she

_____ care of the little ones."

Stella _____ with her husband. She said:

"That's _____. I decide where the children should

_____ to school, where we should live, _____ we

should invest our money, and _____ we should go on

vacation. He _____ how to keep peace in the _____,

how to solve the country's economic _____, and how to

eliminate crime."

Now ask your partner to read the story to you. You listen. Your
partner reads the story again. You fill in the blanks. Your partner
reads the story one more time. You check your work.

After You Read

Comprehension Check

A. Use these words and phrases to help you write a summary of the story.

anniversary	big chores
happy	little chores
friend	I decide
asked	he decides

B. Find the questions that are answered in the story. Answer them first. Then make up your own answers to the other questions. Share your answers with a partner.

1. When did Stella and Joe get married?
2. How many children do Stella and Joe have?
3. Who decides how they should spend their money?
4. Who decides how to eliminate crime?
5. Who decided where they should have the party?

C. Talk or write about these questions.

1. Do you think Stella or Joe really takes care of the big chores? Explain your answer.
2. Why do you think Stella and Joe have been happy together for twenty-five years?
3. What advice would Stella and Joe give to a young couple before their wedding? What advice would you give?

Structure Practice

A. Complete this dialogue using the word should.

Iris: What _____ I do? _____ I go to the

beach or _____ I go to the movies?

Mark: You _____ go to the beach.

Iris: Why _____ I go to the beach?

Mark: You _____ go to the beach because we only have enough money for one ticket, and I want to go to the movies.

Now ask a partner what you should do after school.

B. Complete each sentence using a cardinal number or an ordinal number.

Cardinal numbers are one, two, three, four, five, etc.
Ordinal numbers are first, second, third, fourth, etc.

1. There are _____ people in the room.

2. In two days, I will celebrate my _____ birthday.

3. For the _____ time, please be quiet.

4. Sharon is the _____ person in line.

5. My aunt and uncle will celebrate their _____ wedding anniversary next month.

C. Write the correct form of the verb for each sentence.

Present Tense: 1. I _____ to school by myself.
                   (to walk)

2. He _____ his teachers.
      (to like)

3. He usually _____ me some flowers.
      (to bring)

Past Tense: 1. She _____ in Europe for five years.
                          (to live)

                  2. They _____ to the movies.
                          (to go)

                  3. You _____ apples yesterday.
                          (to buy)

Future Tense: 1. We _____ a pretty song.
                          (to sing)

                  2. It _____ a sunny day.
                          (to be)

                  3. You and I _____ together.
                          (to study)

Problems, Anyone?

Before You Read

A. What do you think of when you see the word <u>graduate</u>? Write some words in the map.

graduate

Now write four sentences about graduating using the ideas from your map.

B. Look at the picture on page 123. Answer the questions.

1. What do you see in the picture?
2. What do you think this story will be about?

C. Look for these words and phrases and underline them in the story. Then write a definition for each one. Use the story for help.

autograph book	to remember
to explain	senior
to graduate	usual
most	to wish

Compare definitions with a partner. Use a dictionary to check the meaning of any word or phrase you disagree about.

D. Match the antonyms (words that have opposite meanings).

1. to remember	a. last
2. first	b. to begin
3. usual	c. almost none
4. to graduate	d. to forget
5. most	e. extraordinary

Problems, Anyone?

Mariko was a senior in high school. She was going to graduate in June. She bought an autograph book. She wanted all her friends to write something in it.

"I want to have a souvenir of all of you," she explained to one friend. "This way, after I graduate, I'll read what you wrote and I will remember you."

Most of her friends wrote the usual things.

> Dear Mariko:
>> U R
>> 2 good
>> <u>2 be</u>
>>
>> 4 gotten

But Sally wrote: "May all your problems be little ones."
Mariko was annoyed.
"Why are you wishing me any problems at all? I don't want big problems or little problems."
"Mariko, you didn't understand my wish. When I say 'little ones,' I mean children."

While You Read

A. As you read, take notes and fill in the chart.

main character	
what she did	
why she did it	
what happened	
why she was annoyed	
what she didn't understand	

Use your notes to help you write a paragraph about Mariko.

B. Think about these questions while you read. Then answer the questions.

1. Who is Mariko?
2. Who is Sally?
3. What do you think about Sally's wish?
4. What would you write in a classmate's autograph book?
5. What souvenirs do you have of your friends?
6. Do you always understand what your friends say to you?
7. Do you ever feel hurt or angry by something a friend says?

After You Read

Comprehension Check

A. Match columns A and B to make sentences about the story.

1. Mariko bought an   a. to graduate in June.
2. May all your problems   b. Sally's wish.
3. She wanted to have   c. autograph book.
4. Mariko was going   d. be little ones.
5. Mariko didn't understand   e. a souvenir of her friends.

B. Choose the best word to complete each sentence.

1. Mariko was a _____ in high school.
   a. junior   b. senior   c. freshman

2. Mariko bought a/an _____.
   a. souvenir   b. notebook   c. autograph book

3. Sally's wish was for _____.
   a. problems   b. friends   c. children

4. Mariko didn't want to have any _____.
   a. problems   b. friends   c. autographs

5. Mariko will _____ her friends when she reads her autograph book.
   a. understand   b. wish   c. remember

C. Fold and staple a few pieces of paper to make an autograph book. Then ask all your classmates to write something in it. Write something in their books, too. When everyone finishes writing, read the autographs in your book. Ask questions if you don't understand a classmate's message. Keep your autograph book as a souvenir of the class.

Write a short paragraph that tells what you think about autograph books. Do you like writing in them? Do you like reading the messages in them? Why or why not?

Structure Practice

A. Change each sentence to the future tense. Follow the example.

Example: Mariko bought an autograph book.
Mariko will buy an autograph book.

1. Mariko was a senior in high school.
2. Mariko graduated in June.
3. Most of her friends wrote the usual things.
4. Mariko read her friends' messages.
5. Mariko remembered her friends.

B. Rewrite this wish in a sentence:

U R
2 good
2 be
_____
4 gotten

Underline the homonyms in the sentence.

C. Write the plural of each noun. Then write a sentence using each plural.

1. knife
2. child
3. man

4. woman
5. tooth

Can you think of any more irregular plurals?

Story 19

If I Knew You Were Coming . . .

Before You Read

A. What do you think of when you see the phrase <u>surprise party</u>? Write some words in the map.

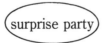

Now write a short paragraph about surprise parties using the ideas from your map.

B. Look at the picture on page 130. Answer the questions.

1. What do you see in the picture?
2. What do you think the girls are going to do?

C. Match each word or phrase with its definition. Check your
work with a partner. Look at the story if you need help.

1. to celebrate	a. to do something unexpected
2. to enter	b. a set of steps or rungs between two long poles
3. to go out with	c. to do something special
4. to have nerve	d. center
5. I'll bet	e. to go in
6. ladder	f. an instrument for work
7. middle	g. I'm almost sure
8. note	h. to have courage (used in a negative way)
9. to surprise	i. to date
10. tool	j. a little written message

D. Choose the word that best completes each sentence.

1. A hammer, nails, pliers, a saw, and a screwdriver are

    _____.

    a. tools   b. fools   c. pools

2. A little letter is a _____.
    a. small   b. short   c. note

3. Something you climb to help you reach high things is a

    _____.

    a. back   b. ladder   c. elevator

4. When something is in the middle, it is in the _____.
    a. center   b. stomach   c. waist

5. Harry came for the weekend without telling us. He has

    _____.

    a. three children   b. two suitcases   c. some nerve

If I Knew You Were Coming . . .

1

Sam usually worked on Sunday, but one Sunday he had nothing to do. He decided to visit his girlfriend Betty. It was his birthday, and he wanted to celebrate.

Betty decided to surprise Sam. She went to his place to prepare a little party for him. She went over with Sam's sister, who had the key. When Betty entered the apartment, she saw that Sam wasn't working that day. His work shoes were near the bed; his work clothes were on the chair; and his tools were near the table. Where was Sam?

"Why didn't he call me?" wondered Betty. "Maybe he doesn't love me anymore. That's it. I'll bet he went out with another girl. He has some nerve. I'm not going to give him a party."

She told Sam's sister that she felt sick and went home.

2

Meanwhile, Sam arrived at Betty's house.

"Where's Betty?" Sam wondered. "She said she was going to be home. Where did she go? Why isn't she home? Why didn't she tell me last night? She knows I usually work on Sundays. Maybe she doesn't love me anymore. I'll bet she went out with another boy. She has some nerve. I won't even leave her a note."

3

The next day, Sam and Betty saw each other in school.

"I'm so angry at you," said Sam. "I don't want to see you anymore. I went to visit you yesterday, but you weren't home. Why didn't you call me to tell me you were going out? I'll bet you went out with another guy."

"Why," said Betty, "because you weren't at work, and you weren't home either. I went to your apartment with your sister, to give you a surprise party. 'Sam should be at work,' I thought to myself. But no! Your work clothes and tools were in your apartment. You have some nerve thinking I went out with another guy. I'll bet you were out with another girl. I don't want to see you anymore."

"Wait a minute," said Sam. "I can explain everything. When I came home, I thought someone was in my house. I saw the ladder in the middle of the room, and I saw a bag of decorations on the table. Was that you?"

"Yes, it was," said Betty angrily.

4   "Listen, Betty. I'm really sorry I thought you went out with another guy. I just wanted to surprise you."

"And I just wanted to surprise you," said Betty. "Let's forget the whole thing, and remember next time to telephone before we decide to 'surprise' each other."

"Good idea!" replied Sam. "If I only knew you were coming. . . ."

While You Read

A. While you read, complete this chart. Put an X in the "yes" or "no" column for each person.

	Sam		Betty	
	yes	no	yes	no
usually worked on Sunday				
had a key to Sam's apartment				
was having a birthday				
wanted to prepare a surprise party				
was at work				
was at home				
was sick				
was angry				
went out with another girl				
went out with another boy				
will forget the whole thing				

B. Read the story again. Stop after each section to answer the questions.

Section 1. Where did Betty go? Why? Why did she leave?

Section 2. Where did Sam go? What did he do? Why?

Section 3. Where did Betty and Sam see each other? What did they say?

Section 4. What did Betty and Sam decide? Will they see each other again?

After You Read

Comprehension Check

A. Choose the best answer to complete each sentence.

1. Betty knew Sam wasn't working because _____.
   a. she saw his work clothes and tools
   b. his work clothes were gone
   c. his work clothes were dirty

2. Sam didn't call Betty because _____.
   a. he went on a date
   b. he didn't love her anymore
   c. he went to her house

3. Sam _____ worked on Sundays.
   a. always   b. sometimes   c. usually

4. Betty and Sam were _____ each other.
   a. surprised at   b. angry with   c. proud of

5. They decided to _____.
   a. forget each other
   b. forget their argument
   c. forget Sam's birthday

B. Number these sentences so they tell the story about Sam and Betty. Then check your work with a partner.

_____ She saw that Sam wasn't working, and she was angry that he wasn't spending the day with her.

_____ Sam and Betty decided not to surprise each other anymore.

_____ Betty wanted to give Sam a surprise birthday party.

_____ Sam went to Betty's house and was angry that she wasn't there.

_____ She went to Sam's apartment to put up decorations.

C. Talk or write about these questions.

1. Is it a good idea to visit people without telling them you're coming? Why or why not?
2. Do you think Betty really felt sick? Explain your answer.
3. What do you think about Sam's and Betty's behavior? Did they have good reason to be angry with each other? Why or why not?
4. What would you do in this situation if you were Sam's sister? How could you help Sam and Betty?
5. Do you like surprise parties? Why or why not?

Structure Practice

A. Change these sentences to the negative form. Follow the example.

Example: Sam had a sister.
Sam didn't have a sister.

1. Sam worked on Sunday.
2. Betty went to visit him.
3. Betty was angry at Sam.
4. Sam saw a ladder in the room.
5. There was a bag of decorations on the table.

B. Change these sentences to question form. Follow the example.

Example: Sam worked on Sunday.
Did Sam work on Sunday?

1. Sam wasn't at home.
2. He went out.
3. Betty and Joan came to visit.
4. They wanted to surprise Sam.
5. The surprise didn't work out.

C. Change this paragraph to the future tense.

Sam worked on Saturday, but on Sunday, May 4, he had nothing to do. He visited his girlfriend. It was his birthday, and he wanted to celebrate with her.

 *Story 20*

Something's Fishy Here

Before You Read

A. What do you think of when you see the word <u>restaurant</u>? Write some words in the map.

Now write a short paragraph about restaurants using the ideas from your map.

B. Look at the picture on page 137. Answer the questions.

1. What do you see in the picture?
2. Where are the two boys?
3. What are the boys doing?
4. What are the boys thinking about?
5. What do you think this story will be about?

C. Do you know what these words and phrases mean? Talk about their meanings with a partner. Then use a dictionary to check your work.

comfortable
to explore
to go off
meal
menu

to pack
phrase book
poison
unfortunately
waiter

D. Use the words in activity C to complete these sentences. Change the form of a word if necessary.

1. Since Steve and Mark didn't speak any French, they took a French _____ when they went to Haiti.

2. We eat three _____ a day: breakfast, lunch, and dinner.

3. This looks like an interesting place. Let's _____ it.

4. _____ is something that can make you sick or kill you.

5. The _____ brought Steve and Mark their food.

6. The hotel room was very _____. It had a shower, a toilet, a sink, and two big beds.

7. The boys _____ to find a good restaurant.

8. Steve and Mark _____ their clothes in suitcases.

9. _____, the boys didn't have their phrase book when they needed it.

10. You can't have ice cream; it's not on the _____.

Something's Fishy Here

Steve and Mark were good friends. They decided to spend their Easter vacation in Haiti. Since they spoke no Creole or French, they took a French phrase book with them and hoped it would help them in difficult situations.

1   The flight was excellent, and the hotel was very comfortable. Each day after breakfast, Steve and Mark packed a picnic lunch and dinner and went off to explore interesting places. After a while, the boys became tired of eating picnic meals and decided to eat a big fish dinner in a good restaurant. Unfortunately, they left their phrase book in the hotel.

They studied the menu carefully. After ten minutes, Steve said to Mark:

"I don't understand this menu."

"Neither do I," said Mark. "I see poison on this menu. Are they crazy here?"

2

"Maybe. They even spelled *poison* wrong. They spelled it p-o-i-s-s-o-n instead of p-o-i-s-o-n. But it must mean the same thing. Maybe we should go to another restaurant. I don't want to eat something that will kill me."

But Mark was tired, so he said:

"There is no other restaurant near here, and I'm tired of walking around the city. Let's order something else instead. It's crowded here, so the food must be good."

The boys looked at the menu again. They finally decided to order steak, although they really wanted fish. Mark called the waiter. The waiter spoke only French and Creole, but the boys just pointed to the word *steak,* and the waiter understood.

As they were eating, they heard some tourists speaking English.

3

"This fish is delicious."

"Yes. I wonder how they prepared it. I must ask the chef for his recipe."

"We're lucky we picked a restaurant that's famous for its fish."

Steve and Mark wondered about what they heard.

"Famous for its fish? There was no fish on the menu!" said Mark.

Finally, Steve said:

"I'm confused. Let's ask them what the story is! I'm beginning to feel very stupid."

Mark felt stupid, too. He said:

"I'll ask. Excuse me, how did you order fish when it wasn't on the menu?"

"Sure it's on the menu. It's right here. *Poisson.*"

4

The boys exclaimed:

"*Poisson.* That's poison! We were wondering how a restaurant like this could have poison on the menu."

The tourists laughed. One of them said:

"No. *Poisson* is French for *fish.*"

Steve and Mark laughed.

"The joke's on us. We thought *poisson* was poison, and so we ordered steak."

While You Read

A. Keep a mini-literature log. After you read each section of the
story, write a sentence that tells your reaction. Follow one of
these examples or make up your own ''I'' sentences:

> I wonder why...
> I like the way...
> I want to know...
> I'm surprised that ...
> If I were ...

B. 1. Complete this time line to show the order of the events in the story.

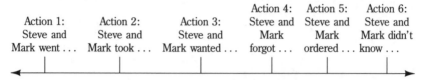

Action 1: Steve and Mark went ...   Action 2: Steve and Mark took ...   Action 3: Steve and Mark wanted ...   Action 4: Steve and Mark forgot ...   Action 5: Steve and Mark ordered ...   Action 6: Steve and Mark didn't know ...

2. Share your time line with a partner. Then take turns telling the story about Steve and Mark. Use your time lines for help.

After You Read

Comprehension Check

A. Write **T** if the sentence is true and **F** if it is false. Correct the sentence if it is false.

1. Steve and Mark went to France for their vacation.
2. There weren't many people in the restaurant.
3. The waiter spoke English and Creole.
4. Steve and Mark ordered steak.
5. The restaurant was famous for its steak.

B. Answer the questions with a partner.

1. What language did Steve and Mark speak?
2. What did Steve and Mark do each day?
3. What did Steve and Mark want to eat at the restaurant?
4. Why did Steve and Mark order steak?
5. How did Steve and Mark feel?

C. After they leave the restaurant, Steve and Mark talk about what happened in the restaurant. What did they learn? What will they do in the future? Role-play the conversation with a partner.

Structure Practice

A. Here is a list of the verbs in the story. Write them in the following tenses. Use the third person singular form.

Infinitive	Present	Present Continuous	Past	Past Continuous	Future
to be	is	is being	was	was being	will be
to decide					
to spend					
to speak					
to take					
to hope					
to pack					
to go					
to explore					
to become					
to eat					
to leave					
to study					
to understand					
to see					
to say					
to spell					

Infinitive	Present	Present Continuous	Past	Past Continuous	Future
to mean					
to want					
to reply					
to laugh					
to think					
to order					
to wonder					
to have					

B. Make a chart of the pronouns you studied in this book.

Subject	Object	Possessive	Reflexive
I			
you			
he			
she			
it			
we			
you			
they			

C. Put together words from each column to make five sentences.
Then compare sentences with a partner.

John	quickly	ate	into	the big	steak
They	slowly	ran	to	the crowded	dog
Steve	sadly	finished	a	the gray	bus stop
My sister	hungrily	walked	to	delicious	homework
The children	finally	said goodbye	their	difficult	store

The Greedy Dog

Before You Read

A. What do you think of when you see the word <u>folktale</u>? Write some words in the map.

Now write a short paragraph about folktales using the ideas from your map.

B. Look at the picture on page 144. Answer the questions.

1. What do you see in the picture?
2. What do you think this story will be about?
3. Think about the title. Does the title help explain the picture?
4. Do you know any folktales about a greedy dog?

C. Read these sentences with a partner. Can you guess the meanings of the underlined words? Use a dictionary if you need help.

Definitions

1. Sam is very helpful. He always <u>volunteers</u> to do the hardest jobs.

_____

Definitions

2. Don't be <u>greedy</u>. Save some
    cookies for your brother.
    _____

3. Did you read Andy's book
    report on *A Wrinkle in
    Time?* It <u>sounds like</u> a good
    book.
    _____

4. Hector <u>raises</u> rabbits. Then
    he sells them to people who
    want pets.
    _____

5. When Janet saw the bus
    coming, she <u>grabbed</u> her
    backpack and ran to the bus
    stop.
    _____

6. Josie smiled at her <u>reflection</u>
    in the store window.
    _____

7. Tim looked at himself in the
    <u>mirror</u> and combed his hair.
    _____

8. Susan turned off the TV.
    "What a sad movie," she
    <u>sighed</u>.
    _____

9. I learned a lot from that
    story. I really agree with its
    <u>moral</u>.
    _____

10. Jacques is <u>worried about</u> the
    science test next week, so
    he is studying now.
    _____

D. Complete each sentence with a word or phrase from the
underlined words in activity C. Change the form of the word
if necessary.

1. My parents _____ five children.

2. Phillip needed help in math, so I _____ to study
    with him.

3. I looked at my _____ in the _____.

4. Quick! _____ the books before they fall.

The Greedy Dog

On Friday afternoon the students in Mr. Perez's class decided to tell some folktales from their native countries.

Mr. Perez asked, "Who wants to volunteer?"

Nii waved his arm eagerly. "I want to tell a story about a greedy dog."

"Sounds like my dog," laughed Jun. "He is always running after food."

"I like cats better than dogs," whispered Anna to Carmen, who was sitting next to her.

"Okay, class," said Mr. Perez, "let's be quiet and let Nii tell the story."

"Well," began Nii, "there was once a man who raised dogs. One day he went out and left the door of his house opened. While he was gone, one of the dogs went into the house and climbed on the

table. The dog grabbed some meat in his teeth. Then he saw his reflection in the mirror. The dog thought, 'Oh, oh! There is a friend with some more meat. I'm going to get that meat, too!' He jumped at the mirror, and the mirror crashed down on him. His cuts were so bad that he died.''

''The poor dog!'' sighed Tanya.

''The moral of this story is that you should be satisfied with what you have,'' said Nii.

''I'm worried about my dog,'' exclaimed Jun. ''He doesn't understand that moral! I'm going right home after school and taking down all the mirrors in the house.''

While You Read

A. As you read, take notes and fill in the charts.

Mr. Perez's class

What did the students decide?	
Who volunteered?	
What story did he want to tell?	
How did Jun feel after he heard the story?	
What did he want to do?	

The folktale

The man raised . . .	
The dog grabbed . . .	
The dog saw . . .	
The dog tried to get . . .	
His cuts were so bad that . . .	
The moral is . . .	

B. Keep a mini-literature log. After you read the story, write a paragraph that tells your reactions. Follow one of these examples or make up your own "I" sentence to begin.

> I think that . . .
> I'm surprised that . . .
> If I were . . .

After You Read

Comprehension Check

A. Sit with a partner and tell or write the folktale about the greedy dog. Use the information from your chart above.

B. Talk or write about these questions.

1. What is a folktale?
2. Why do you think the students in Mr. Perez's class tell folktales?

3. Do you think the story Nii tells really happened?
4. What is the moral of this folktale? Do you agree with it?
5. Why was Jun worried? Would you be worried if you had a dog like Jun's?
6. Do you think this folktale is about dogs' behavior or people's behavior?
7. What country do you think this folktale is from? Is there a folktale like this from your native country?

C. Do you know any folktales? Sit with a partner. Tell your partner a folktale from your native country or any other country. Think about these questions after you tell the story.

1. Does your folktale have a moral? What is it?
2. Do you agree with the moral? Why or why not?
3. Is your story similar to your partner's? Tell one thing that's similar and one thing that's different.
4. Ask someone at home to tell you a folktale from your native country. Share it with your class.

Structure Practice

A. Change each sentence to the future tense.

1. The students in Mr. Perez's class told some folktales.
2. The man raised dogs.
3. The dog grabbed the meat.
4. Jun went home after school.
5. Jun took down all the mirrors in the house.

B. Here are some answers. Ask a question for each answer. Follow the example.

Example: Nii volunteered to tell a story.
Who volunteered to tell a story?

1. Anna likes cats better than dogs.
2. He grabbed some meat.
3. He saw his reflection in the mirror.
4. Jun is worried about his dog.
5. He is going right home.

C. Find five verbs in the story. Write a new sentence for each verb. Practice using different tenses.

Alphabetized Vocabulary by Page

A

across   50
(to) adjust   28
(to) agree   1
alarm system   80
anniversary   114
(to) announce   43
annoyed (to be...)   1
anyway   86
(to) approach   21
around the corner   101
as a result   95
as long as   109
autograph book   122
awkward   64

B

bandage   72
(to) be annoyed   1
(to) be greedy   143
(to) be satisfied   22
(to) be upset   9
(to) to be worried about   143
beautiful   50
behavior   22
blind date   64
block   101
by herself/himself   101

C

camping   80
can't stand   87
(to) celebrate   128
charge   22
(to) cheat   43
(to) check in   9
cheer up   108
chores   114
classmates   101
comfortable   134
(to) complain   22
(to) concentrate   43
(to) continue   2
counselor   87
crazy   87
crimes   115
crowded   87
curator   72

D

date   109
definitely   28
delicious   109
difficult   9
don't worry   108

E

easy   115
economic   115
eliminate   115
embarrassed   16
(to) enjoy   50
(to) enter   128
everyone   2
(to) exchange   35
exhausted   80
(to) explain   122
(to) explore   134

F

(to) fool   35
frightened   80
front   2
funny look   50

G

generous   57
(to) get up   2
(to) go off   134
(to) go out with   128
(to) go steady   64
(to) grab   143
(to) graduate   122
great   28
greedy (to be)   143
(to) guess   80

H

handsome   36
(to) hate   28
(to) have deep meaning   72
(to) have nerve   128
high marks   108

(to) hitchhike   58
hot   2
huge   16

I

icy   50
identical   36
identification   80
I'll bet   128
inside out   101
instead of   58
(to) invest   115

K

(to) keep an eye on   80
keyed up   80
kindness   58

L

ladder   128
leave me alone   22
left   57
lobby   101
lucky   16

M

(to) make an appointment   101
(to) make the rounds   72
(to) manage   115
meal   134
menu   134
metro   16
middle   128
mirror   143
mismatch   64
(to) miss   95, 109
moral   143
most   122

N

nearly   28
next   87
noise   2
note   128
(to) notice   28

O

on time (to be...)   101
out of order (to be...)   95
over a/an   101

P

(to) pack   134
palm tree   109
phrase book   134
(to) pick on   28
pocket   50
(to) point   50
poison   134
practical joke   36
(to) pretend   22
problems   28
(to) promise   109
promptly   80
(to) pull into   95

Q

quiet   2

R

(to) raise   143
rear   75
(to) receive   95
reflection   143
(to) refuse   58
relationship   64

(to) remember   122
(to) review   72
roomier   87

S

satisfied   22, 95
satisfied (to be...)   22
(to) save some for a rainy day   58
scale   9
schedule   28
seats   22
senior   122
set   80
(to) shout   22
(to) show up   101
(to) shrug one's shoulders   50
shy   109
(to) sigh   143
(to) sit back   95
slim   36
(to) solve   87
(to) sound like   143
souvenir   58
(to) spend   58
(to) stay   115
store   50
(to) stutter   36
such a (painting)   72
(to) summarize   36
(to) surprise   128

T

(to) take care of   115
(to) take one's time   9
(to) talk   2
teenagers   28
(to) tell apart   36
(to) threaten   87
tool   128
tourist   16
transportation authority   95
twins   36

U

unfortunately   134
upset (to be...)   9
usual   122
usually   95

V

volunteers   142

W

waiter   134
(to) wander   43
(to) warn   43
wheelchair   22
while   50
wise   87
(to) wish   122
(to) wonder   58
worried about (to be)   143